RESOLVING THE UNHEALTHY AND ABUSIVE MARRIAGE PANDEMIC

God's Transforming Grace

Safe, Secure and Loved

DISCLAIMER

This book is written and intended to be a perspective for faith leaders to understand the different types of marriages, how to identify, support, and guide victims of domestic abuse in a safe way, and how to recognize and deal with an abuser. The book is Biblically based on the teachings, character, attributes, and majesty of God, Jesus, and the Holy Spirit.

The author, Darla Colinet, CEO of God's Transforming Grace™, assumes no responsibility for how a reader responds to or uses any information provided in this book. She is not a counselor, therapist, or psychologist and does not intend this book as any form of therapy or treatment. Nothing contained in this book shall constitute professional advice or treatment.

Darla is a Certified Professional Life Coach, (CPC), and a Certified Christian Coach, (CCRC).

ISBN Paperback   979-8-9855165-2-4
        Ebook 979-8-9855165-3-1

God's Transforming Grace
Safe, Secure and Loved

Printed in the United States of America

RESOLVING THE UNHEALTHY AND ABUSIVE MARRIAGE PANDEMIC

A FAITH LEADER'S ESSENTIAL TRAINING
TO IDENTIY, SUPPORT, AND GUIDE VICTIMS

DARLA COLINET
Author and Consultant

This Fundamental Education Is for:

Faith leaders, including pastors, teachers, mentors, ministry and group leaders, and people who have first contact with believers struggling in their marriage.

Faith leaders desiring to learn how to identify and support believers struggling in a toxic-abusive marriage need this education! Unless you learn the source of a person's confusion about love and marriage and the definition, types, and signs of abuse, you may have trouble identifying if their marriage has unhealthy aspects that can be worked out or if it is toxic-abusive. Until you know what type of marriage they have and their definition of love, you will not know how to help.

The detailed aspects of Christ's healthy love, the types of marriages, and the unhealthy and toxic-abusive marriage dynamics are not often taught at great lengths in the church or Bible schools. Missing these realities leaves faith leaders unaware and unprepared. Although your heart wants to help, you can only do what you know. And you may cause more harm than good!

A faith leader is usually the first person a believer contacts when struggling in their marriage. How we approach them and what we say have a paramount influence on their decisions and lives. Anyone seen in the place of authority or as a faith leader must be aware and ready for people coming to them for help.

This fundamental education shows us how believers get confused about love and marriage and God's answers. It will equip us with the knowledge we need to identify the type of marriage the person is in and how to help them. We will understand our role and know how to access and recommend our local resources. Without good direction, people lose their way; the more wise counsel you follow, the better your chances. (Proverbs 11:14, MSG)

> Pay careful attention to yourselves and to all the flock, in which the Holy Spirit has made you overseers, to care for the church of God, which he obtained with his own blood. (Acts 20:28, ESV)

Together, we can reduce or eliminate the number of toxic-abusive marriages in the church by equipping faith leaders and believers with a clear path to learn what it means to love like Jesus. Let's work with Jesus and begin!

Educational Objectives Overview

Users Guide

Structure of Course Language

We have identified the victim as the woman or wife to simplify the education and to reflect the facts that women are primarily the victims. When the education discusses unhealthiness or toxic abuse, it will refer to the unhealthy one or abuser as male.

Make no mistake, men are abused, too, and I acknowledge their victimization. I intend no disrespect or discounting of their pain. If you are an abused man, the same teachings and Christ's design of healthy love also apply to you. Whether the abuser is male or female, abuse is never acceptable or God's will.

Foundation for Education

God's Word and the life of Jesus Christ are the primary foundations for this education. Every effort has been made to follow God's truth in context and Christ's loving example. Their foundations give us an unchangeable standard and compass to follow, which is vital as we all have individual perspectives, ideas, standards, and beliefs.

The education also encompasses Darla's experiences, information gathered from books on God's love and abuse, talks with numerous counselors, and the conversations she had with hundreds of Christian women struggling to understand or fix their marriages.

These lessons and revelations can help faith leaders understand why believers are confused about their understanding of love versus what they hear from the pulpit or read in the Bible. We can meet believers where they are, just like Jesus did.

If believers don't know what it truly means to love like Jesus or to be loved like him, and the definition, types, and signs of abuse, how can they thrive in Christ's exceptional love?

Statistics

Every effort has been made to find the most current statistics used in this education manual. All references will be in the endnotes.

Caution: Self-Grace

You have taken a big step to learn how to meet believers where they are and show them Christ's healthy love. Each faith leader comes with their unique definition and understanding of love. You can't change how you tried to help believers in the past. If you discover during this study that you said or did something unhealthy or harmful in the past, ask Jesus for forgiveness first, then give yourself forgiveness and grace.

We can only do what we know. You didn't know all of these facts and realities before this education. As you learn God's truth, you will know how to show believers how they can love like Jesus. To grow and move forward, you cannot live in the past. So, forgive yourself, live in Christ's grace, and let's move forward.

How to Get the Best Results with This Education

We all come to this education from different perspectives, experiences, understandings, and beliefs about love and marriage. This education is your opportunity to explore what you have come to accept as "normal" in a marriage or assumptions you have made about love and marriage as a Christian. Hearing the facts about the types of marriages and abuse may raise questions, objections, or emotions.

Don't be surprised if your emotions or memories are triggered, especially if you have a loved one who was abused or you are a survivor. Go through this book in a safe space. If you need to take a break or talk to a counselor, do what is necessary, and then come back. This is a difficult topic.

Allow yourself to see what information you have not been taught about love, marriage, and abuse that may have subconsciously kept you blind to identifying and understanding abuse. When we use God's word and Christ's life as our unchanging compass and standard we can find unity and Christ's clear path to follow. Let Jesus show you his truth.

Jesus taught us to meet people where they are in compassion and to share his truth. The more we study each section and participate in the class exercise, the more we will learn from this class. Let's help believers grow and break the cycle of unhealthy and toxic-abusive marriages within the church by getting equipped to fight this battle.

It is also important for you to understand what our role and responsibilities are as faith leaders.

> Faith Leaders, it's not our job to fix, heal, save, or professionally counsel believers coming to us for help. It's our responsibility to know how to listen to them without dismissal, judgment, and condemnation and determine what kind of help they need and provide it in Christ's love.

Rather, speaking the truth in love, we are to grow up in every way into him who is the head, into Christ.

(Eph. 4:15, ESV)

Let us pray. Lord, help us open ourselves up to this education because we desire to help believers thrive in Christ's love in a happy, healthy marriage. Our goal is to help confused, hurting believers understand Your healthy, loving partnership design for marriage and how to live in it. We pray that You help us confidently provide a clear path for all believers to thrive in Christ's love in practical ways, whether they are single or married. Lord, let everyone know that this is a safe space for us to share and learn.

May God bless us with His wisdom, knowledge, understanding, and discernment during our time together. Amen.

PART 1

ALL ABOUT MARRIAGE: FACTS, SOURCES OF CONFUSION, AND GOD'S DESIGN OF MARRIAGE

Realities of Unhealthy and Toxic-abusive Marriages in the Church

A Picture of a Believer Struggling in Their Marriage

In 1982, at eighteen, I married my Lutheran high school sweetheart. I hoped and prayed that I had found my true love and that I would have the happy family I'd dreamed of. However, my dream quickly turned into a nightmare.

Three months into my marriage, my husband got drunk, pushed me around, and degraded me. I stood up to him only to have a shotgun shoved into my mouth. My husband told me that he would blow my head off if I ever stood up to him again or tried to leave.

Although I was filled with fear, I waited for my husband to fall asleep. Once he did, I snuck into the kitchen to call my parents. My dad answered the phone. I told him what happened. He said, "You are married under a covenant with God. You've made your bed; now you have to lie in it."

My dad's abandonment and betrayal shattered my heart. If he wouldn't help me, what options did I have? I thought that maybe this was God's will, somehow. But the abuse continued over the next year, and I struggled to believe it was God's will.

I kept going to church and looking for answers. I gathered up my courage and met with the pastor. After I told him what was going on, he prayed with me to be more understanding, submissive, and willing to turn the other cheek, forgive and forget, and stay married because God hates divorce.

I walked away from the church and God for several years and dove into self-help books. I kept trying to fix myself and my marriage. I didn't realize that I was not the cause of abuse but a victim.

Over the next twelve years, the abuse extended to my children, and I left several times. With my husband's promises to change, listening to the advice and pressure of other Christians, and my dad's plea not to make God mad because God hates divorce, I returned. After thirteen long years and horrific abuse, I was pushed to my limit.

I found a safe place for my children, and I made one last plea to my husband. The last thing I remembered was his hands around my throat, choking me until I was unconscious. I awoke and lay still until I knew that I was alone. I jumped up enraged, yelling, "God, either you stop this tonight, or I will."

I went to the gun cabinet, pulled out a shotgun, and loaded it. I sat in the chair facing the back door, waiting for my husband to return. The darkness of my pain and rage overwhelmed me as snapshots of thirteen years of abuse rolled through my mind like a movie. I saw no way out, so I waited.

The sunlight peeking through the window in the door woke me up. At that moment, I realized I had a shotgun in my hands, and I was ready to kill. I cried out to God for help again. Deep in my heart, I heard God say, "I've made a way. Run. This is not love."

As I ran to the door, I remembered reading about a pastor in the local newspaper who was being condemned because he supported his daughter getting a divorce from her abusive husband. I decided to talk with him and drove to his church. The pastor had me read about marriage in Ephesians and in 1 Corinthians 13:4-7. He asked me to replace the word love in the Corinthians passage with my husband's name. As I read these verses, I realized that God's love was not the love I had experienced in my marriage or life.

While I talked and prayed with the pastor about God's truths, I identified some of the lies I had believed. God's truth set me on a course to seek Jesus more. However, I endured another two abusive marriages to "Christian" men that ended in divorce before I put all of Christ's love and God's truth together and broke free from the cycle of abuse.

Sadly, from 1982, my story is not much different from the hundreds of stories I have heard and read over the last few years. The record number of calls from believers and non-believers to the church for help during COVID has brought to light the silent pandemic of unhealthy and toxic-abusive marriages that have been in our churches for centuries.

As history has proven, the silent pandemic of unhealthy and abusive marriages within our congregations will not go away. The question faith leaders must ask ourselves is what Jesus would want us to do to help the victims. We don't have to be professional counselors or psychologists. We just have to be equipped to be able to identify victims, know how to give spiritual support, teach them the aspects of Christ's love, and help with referrals for church and community resources.

The only way to transform our love into Christ's and stop living in unhealthy or abusive behaviors in our marriages is to learn all the aspects of Christ's perfect love and implement them in our lives every day.

It is NEVER God's will for any type of unhealthiness or abuse to reside in a Christian marriage. To address these problems, let's look at the facts and statistics of abuse.

Facts and Statistics about Unhealthiness and Abuse in Christian Marriages

Unhealthiness and abuse statistics within Christian marriages are the same as in secular marriages.

> 47 percent (30 percent women and 17 percent men) of the population has been abused or is currently being abused, according to the National Coalition Against Domestic Violence.[1]

Over the last few years, many studies have been done within congregations that help us see this silent pandemic in the church. Dr. Kristin Aune of Coventry University, who led the research at Coventry University and the University of Leicester for the Christian Charity Restored, states:

> Domestic abuse happens in churches too. A quarter of the people we heard from told us they had, for example, been physically hurt by their partners, sexually assaulted, emotionally manipulated, or had money withheld from them. This includes 12 women who have experienced between 10 and 20 abusive behaviors and six women who are currently in relationships where they fear for their lives. . . . Only two in seven churchgoers felt their church was adequately equipped to deal with a disclosure of abuse.[2]

Dr. Aune gives us a glimpse into the real lives of churchgoers that should bring us to our knees. Why are people claiming to love and follow Christ living in unhealthiness and abuse in their "Christian" marriages? Why can't believers struggling in their toxic-abusive marriages find help? It's clear that what faith leaders have been doing for centuries has not worked. So, how can we start changing these realities for the victims in our churches?

> Lifeway Research conducted a study of 1000 Protestant pastors in the summer of 2018. A staggering 54% percent of pastors surveyed said that they are either NOT trained at all, or insufficiently trained, to handle domestic violence issues. [3]

> An overwhelming majority of the faith leaders surveyed (74%) underestimate the level of sexual and domestic violence experienced within their congregations. There was encouragement: 81% of pastors said they would take appropriate action to reduce sexual and domestic violence if they had the education and resources to do so—revealing a great opportunity to turn this uncertain and

1. National Coalition Against Domestic Violence (NCADV). https://ncadv.org/STATISTICS

2. https://www.anglicannews.org/news/2018/03/domestic-abuse-happens-in-churches-too-new-research-highlights-church-goers-experience.aspx ACNS Anglican Communion News Service, Domestic abuse happens in churches too: new research highlights churchgoers' experience, Posted March 21, 2018, 2:47 PM.

3. https://www.agapemoms.com/blog/2018/8/31/silent-epidemic-of-domestic-abuse-violence-christian-church-statistics

unprepared group into powerful advocates for prevention, intervention, and healing

Most of these facts are pre-COVID. From my personal experience of working with many Christian women in unhealthy and toxic-abusive marriages, I can tell you that the reported number (30%) of women being abused is very low. Every woman's shelter in Colorado's Front Range area has been full for the past two years, and they have a waiting list. According to Alternatives to Violence, the numbers of Christian women seeking help in Loveland, Colorado, have doubled since COVID hit: "Domestic violence cases increased by 25-33% globally in 2020. Nearly 20 people per minute."[4]

Most victims of abuse, especially if they are believers, will seek help from a faith leader before another professional because they think it is safer. However, when victims share their reality, the truth is often so hard and horrible to imagine that most victims are discounted, told they are the problem, heaped with spiritual abuse, or put into danger because the faith leader asks the abuser what is going on. When faith leaders respond in dismissive and condemning ways, who can the Christian victims trust or turn to?

I would like to believe that the incorrect handling of the victims is primarily due to unawareness and lack of education of faith leaders. However, being unequipped only further devastates the victims. They feel betrayed, abandoned, and left to try and understand what is going on and to find a way out themselves. Hurting victims is not the words or actions of Jesus Christ.

God's word is the light in the dark places of unhealthiness and toxic abuse. Jesus showed us that he approached everything in love by focusing on the heart. We must know how to provide spiritual teaching and nonjudgmental support, regardless of the believer's decision to stay in the marriage, separate, or divorce. Christ's disciples need our help, support, and teaching on love and marriage according to God's truth, not primarily through a secular foundation that keeps them independent of God.

As faith leaders, we are in a position to influence and help people. Unless we step up and teach believers Christ's definition of love and marriage and facts about healthy, unhealthy, and toxic-abusive marriages, the unhealthy and toxic-abusive marriages in the church will continue. Let's explore how we can equip ourselves to help believers struggling in their marriage by following Christ's lead.

Jesus said several times, "Come, follow me." His was a program of "do what I do," rather than "do what I say." His innate brilliance would have permitted him to put on a dazzling display, but that would have left his followers far behind. He walked and worked with those he was to serve. His was not a long-distance leadership.

---

4. UAB News, Health & Medicine, The pandemic is increasing intimate partner violence. Here is how healthy care can provide help. By Caroline Newman, media contact, Anna Jones.

He was not afraid of close friendships; he was not afraid that proximity to him would disappoint his followers. The leaven of true leadership cannot lift others unless we are with and serve those to be led.

– Spencer W. Kimball

Understanding Key Roadblocks Within the Church

God's Transforming Grace, LLC, helps believers explore their definition of love and how it affects the health of their relationships and marriages and how to deal with abuse according to Scripture. They did a private social media survey asking various faith leaders about their biggest struggles concerning the unhealthy, toxic, and abusive marriages in their congregations. Here are their top three answers.

☑ Divorce

☑ Not equipped and don't know how to approach the subject

☑ Afraid of doing something wrong, so they pray and offer out of context scriptures.

Let's talk briefly about these common roadblocks that have stopped many faith leaders from providing healthy, supportive help.

☑ **Divorce**: Historically, the church has primarily been focused on keeping marriages together, regardless of the destructive, abusive costs to spouses or the children. Many scriptures have been misquoted and misused. Many faith leaders don't believe abuse is a reason for divorce. The result of saving a marriage over the value, health, and life of a person only perpetuates a toxic-abusive marriage and continues the cycle of abuse for children and grandchildren. We will cover divorce in greater detail later

☑ **Not equipped**: The statistics and faith leaders have verified that they didn't receive much, if any, education to identify a marriage with a FEW aspects of unhealthiness from an unhealthy and toxic-abusive marriage. Without knowledge or a professional counselor's education, most faith leaders handle all marriage issues as a "couples" problem and refer them to couples counseling. However, abuse is a choice by the abuser alone to act sinfully against his spouse. The victim does not share in the abuser's choice to sin. Sending an unhealthy or toxic-abusive couple to couples counseling will escalate the abuse and cause more harm. When faith leaders learn the origin of unhealthiness and abuse, the aspects of abuse, and how to overcome it with Christ's love design, this roadblock can be eliminated. We will learn about these aspects in greater detail

☑**Afraid of doing something wrong, so they pray and offer out of context scriptures**: When you don't know how to fix a car, and you don't stop to learn before you tear into an engine, you can do more harm than good. Dealing with the real-life issues of unhealthy and toxic-abusive marriages in the church requires education. When you offer scriptures that you think will help without knowing what a person is dealing with, you can inflict more harm. This process is called spiritual abuse. Spiritual abuse heaps more abuse on the victim, whether intentional or not; abuse has no place in God's love

Although these roadblocks have been around for centuries, they can be torn down, and the captive victims of abuse can be set free. You can identify, help, and support victims in healthy ways by equipping yourself with the right knowledge, understanding, and tools. Thank you for choosing to learn how to end this pandemic with Christ.

The Confusion Believers Have About Love and Marriage

We Can Only Do What We Know

Elephants are smart and strong, so why don't they run away from their trainers? What makes them stay under the control? When an elephant trainer begins to work with a baby elephant, they tie one end of a strong rope around her ankle and tie the other end of the rope to a stake in the ground. If she decides to get up and go on her own, she is stopped when she reaches the end of the rope.

As the elephant grows bigger, the trainer can disconnect the rope from the stake while leaving the loop around the elephant's ankle. The elephant will stay near the trainer and obey his commands because she knows she has more freedom with her trainer than she has on her own. She is bound by her past experiences and can't see the reality of her power.

This same principle is true for us when we look at our current understanding of love. We have all explored, redefined, and experienced the meaning of love at various times in our lives. Some of us say love is a feeling, attitude, words, and actions, but do we know what Jesus says?

How Our Definition and Understanding of Love Is Formed

When people come to faith leaders for help, we must realize they are coming from their current understanding of love, which they think is similar to ours. Likewise, we listen with our understanding of love and experiences, and we think the believer's definition of love is similar to ours. Because billions of people have individual interpretations of love, what is the true definition of love for Christians? How can we recognize it and teach Christ's disciples to live in it?

First, we must acknowledge that we're not born with the understanding and knowledge of God's word or Christ's love design laid out in a clear path. We each formed our original love design without the truth of Christ, which makes it imperfect and broken. Everyone's current definitions and understanding of love have evolved over their lifetime from the following:

☑ Words and messages we heard and believed about ourselves and love

☑ Good and painful love experiences in our relationships

☑ Role models we watched

☑ Actions and words we came to accept as "normal" and "loving"

☑ The world's portrayal of selfish, disrespectful love seen in movies, romance books, pornography, etc.

☑ Beliefs about love, ourselves, others, God, and Jesus Christ

People asking for guidance or help may have been deceived into believing it's okay if someone yells at them, is mean to them, or hurts them as long as they apologize. They might believe they must allow family members to hurt or disrespect them to keep the peace and to be a "good Christian." They might believe that jealousy proves their spouses love them.

Believers might think they must allow their spouses to monitor or control who they talk to or spend time with. These unhealthy and disrespectful beliefs, words, and behaviors are not in Christ's divine love, but many believers don't know it.

Their hearts and intentions are to follow Jesus. But their spiritual knowledge, faith, and abilities to overcome are limited by their beliefs, experiences, and lack of discipleship and education. They only do what they know, just like the adult elephant with the rope around her ankle.

Many believers can assume that when they are saved, Jesus will heal their brokenness and unhealthiness automatically or over time. They may also think that he will instantly teach them to love like him, and their marriages will be great. Not many new believers are told about their responsibility to work with Jesus to learn his ways. They're not taught how to study God's word, to live in Christ's identity and love design, be led by the Holy Spirit, and how to overcome their challenges with Christ.

Many believers are told to love like Jesus and stop their unhealthy and sinful behaviors, but they do not have a healthy reference point from their lives to really understand Christ's healthy love. They don't understand that they can't instantly delete, change, or stop using their imperfect love designs. They don't know where to begin or if it is even possible for them.

Our Ultimate Needs Influence Our Understanding of Love and Decisions

While working in Texas several years ago, I met a young couple at our church just starting a dairy business. They were baffled because so many of their calves were dying in their first week of life.

They sought the wisdom of an experienced dairy farmer. The farmer asked them when they were separating the calves from their mothers. The couple said within a week.

The farmer smiled and said, "The calves need to bond with their mothers and feel loved for at least three weeks or they will lose their will to live." We sheep in God's pasture are the same.

God designed our ultimate needs to feel safe, loved, valued, that we belong, and have a purpose that only He can fill. A void we feel in an ultimate need is designed to ignite our drive to seek God with all of our hearts, minds, and souls. However, Christ's disciples aren't usually taught to seek Him first, so they try to fill a void on their own or with other imperfect people.

The majority of us come into this world having our physical needs met. However, we aren't aware of our ultimate needs and how they guide our thoughts, decisions, beliefs, and behaviors. We may not realize we're operating out of their influence, even though we do our best to follow Jesus.

If you feel love-starved and devalued, like I felt, and you don't learn about Christ's healthy love, you are vulnerable to falling prey to unhealthy, toxic, and abusive people. Your need to feel loved is so deep that you will settle for attention or toxic-abusive love over being alone and abandoned. If people feel unworthy, they will strive to prove their value or earn people's approval to feel valued. Believers need to know about their ultimate needs because the enemy knows their voids, and he will use them to keep believers blind to God's truth.

Without Christ's teachings, believers will act independently of Christ's reign in their lives. Believers will use the methods they have used in the past to try to fulfill their ultimate needs or through other, imperfect people. When believers think they can fulfill what their Creator, God, designed to fill in them through Christ, they are deceived. The drive to feel like you are loved and valued and that you belong and have a purpose at all costs are key aspects in unhealthy and toxic-abusive marriages.

Next, we will look at the design and types of marriages.

All About Marriage

God's Design of Marriage

In the beginning, God defined marriage between one man and one woman. Marriage is not just words exchanged by two people. Marriage is also a covenant (an agreement) between one man, one woman, and God. (Gen. 2:24) God established marriage as a covenant, and if we follow Him, we must follow His marriage design.

God designed marriage to provide a context for a healthy, Holy, equal, loving partnership filled with value, respect, and freedom. It gives each spouse a helping partner to create their family (with or without children), share their sexuality, and walk through life as they honor and serve God.

> This explains why a man leaves his father and mother and is joined to his wife, and the two are united into one. Since they are no longer two but one, let no one split apart what God has joined together. (Matt. 19:5-6, NLT)

Realities of Marriage

All marriages begin with healthy and unhealthy aspects because we are all imperfect. Most Christians enter marriage unaware and unprepared, even though they may have had premarital counseling from their churches. Most believers are not told that they are operating from their imperfect definition of love, and so are their future spouses.

Many believers often assume their definitions and understandings are similar to their spouses because they like the same music, movies, and food. They may also assume they agree on what it means to be a Christian or a Godly wife or husband as well as what respect, forgiveness, and trust looks like, or what is healthy, unhealthy, or toxic-abusive.

They don't take time to evaluate how they and their future spouses handle stress, anger, rejection, disappointment, problem-solving, roles, or power in their marriages. Spouses are also challenged because they weren't instantly downloaded with God's truth when they received Salvation. They weren't born with the knowledge of what a healthy person or a healthy relationship looks like according to Christ's standards.

When two believers come together in their imperfect definitions of love, they must also face the confusion of:

☑ Two personalities

☑ Two sets of imperfect love designs

☑ Two sets of hurts and scars

☑ Two sets of expectations

☑ Two sets of beliefs, definitions, and understandings

☑ Two sets of words and behaviors they believe are okay or normal

Picture each spouse at the end of a rope they call their marriage. When couples struggle between their two imperfect definitions, understandings, and beliefs about love and marriage, a tug-of-wills battle is created. Each spouse tries to pull or operate from their imperfect definition of love because they believe it is best. The tug-of-wills between both spouses' definitions and beliefs is where the unhealthy and toxic-abusive marriage characteristics are revealed.

The most complex relationship in our lives will be with our spouses because we allow them access to our hearts, dreams, wounds, and lives. We invest our love and time doing our best to make our marriages happy and survive life's challenges. But without the knowledge of

God, Christ's love standards, and what is healthy, unhealthy, or toxic-abusive, how can we know if our marriages are following God's design of a healthy, loving partnership?

Faith leaders must never assume that believers understand Christ's healthy love, even if they have been a Christian for decades. Take time to listen. You can tell by their words and fruits.

If believers have never experienced healthy love or healthy relationships, they have no point of reference to understand it. Without experiencing healthy relationships, they may believe it's not possible for them or that they don't deserve to live in Christ's pure love. On top of all of these realities, they don't even know where to begin. If they don't know what is healthy, how can they have healthy marriages?

Before we look at the definitions of a healthy, unhealthy, or toxic-abusive marriage, let's look at the four types of marriage.

Four Types of Marriages

There are four types of marriages. We will focus on the top three types for this teaching.

1. A healthy, loving, equal partnership marriage centered in Christ

2. An unhealthy marriage can be healed if both spouses surrender and work with Christ

3. A toxic-abusive dictatorship marriage

4. Roommates or marriage in name, for convenience, or for legal purposes

Definitions of Healthy, Unhealthy, and Toxic-Abusive

It is a faith leader's privilege and honor to be the extension of Christ and his love in this world. It is also our responsibility to teach believers about God's design of marriage as a partnership so they can thrive in healthy, respectful, loving marriages. To ensure we are all unified in our definitions, we will use Webster's definitions for healthy, unhealthy, and toxic. We will use the National Coalition Against Domestic Violence for abuse.

☑ **Healthy:** good physical condition, well, flourishing, strong, and the ability to adjust and thrive. These conditions cover our body, mind, emotional health, and spirit

☑ **Unhealthy:** harmful, detrimental, destructive, and damaging to a healthy mind, body, emotions, and spirit

☑ **Toxic:** poisonous, dangerous, destructive, harmful, unsafe, malignant, abusive, and deadly

☑ **Abusive**: the willful intimidation, coercion, manipulation, battery, physical or sexual assault, and/or other abusive behavior used in a systematic pattern of power and control over a partner in an intimate relationship. Abuse is delivered in verbal, mental, emotional, financial, electronic, religious, physical, ethnic, and sexual ways[5]

☑ Note: abuse can happen in every kind of relationship as well

☑ Abuse is a learned behavior. It is not an illness or condition. Abuse is a choice to perpetually sin against God and others, which is not Christ's love

To help you see the differences in each type of marriage, let's look at a loving partnership in Christ first.

A Healthy, Loving, Equal Partnership Marriage

God's design for marriage and Christ's example of love is a healthy, loving, equal partnership marriage. The picture of this marriage above reveals both spouses' commitment to keep Christ first and work together. Both spouses follow the two greatest commandments and work with Jesus to grow the fruits of the Holy Spirit. "Love, joy, peace, patience, kindness, goodness, faithfulness, gentleness, and self-control." (Gal. 5:22-23, NIV)

> Wives, understand and support your husbands in ways that show your support for Christ. The husband provides leadership to his wife the way Christ does to his church, not by domineering but by cherishing. So, just as the church submits

---

5. National Coalition Against Domestic Violence

to Christ as he exercises such leadership, wives should likewise submit to their husbands.

Husbands, go all out in your love for your wives, exactly as Christ did for the church—a love marked by giving, not getting. Christ's love makes the church whole. His words evoke her beauty. Everything he does and says is designed to bring the best out of her, dressing her in dazzling white silk, radiant with holiness. And that is how husbands ought to love their wives. They're really doing themselves a favor—since they're already "one" in marriage.

No one abuses his own body, does he? No, he feeds and pampers it. That's how Christ treats us, the church, since we are part of his body. And this is why a man leaves father and mother and cherishes his wife. No longer two, they become "one flesh." This is a huge mystery, and I don't pretend to understand it all. What is clearest to me is the way Christ treats the church. And this provides a good picture of how each husband is to treat his wife, loving himself in loving her, and how each wife is to honor her husband. (Eph. 5:22-33, MSG)

In a healthy, equal partnership marriage, both spouses are committed to working together when they struggle over an occasional (once or twice a year) unhealthy characteristic or issue of money, children, jobs, an illness, or some past or unexpected problem. They are willing to give more if their spouse needs it or do whatever is necessary. They willingly live in repentance concerning anything they need to change to honor their spouse and follow God completely. They value and treat one another as if they were each Christ in the flesh.

To see the characteristics of a healthy marriage, let's look at the following Healthy Relationship Equality table. Notice how in a God and Christ-centered marriage, each person has equal value, respect, voice, and the freedom and power to choose. All of the healthy, loving elements dwell in Christ's love.

HEALTHY RELATIONSHIP EQUALITY

	EQUAL PARTNERSHIP	
NEGOTIATION AND FAIRNESS Seeking mutually satisfying resolutions to conflict. Free to say no and have healthy boundaries. Accepting changes. Being willing to compromise.	E Q U A L	**NON-THREATENING BEHAVIOR** Talking and acting respectfully, so each partner feels safe and comfortable expressing themselves and doing things.
ECONOMIC PARTNERSHIP Making money decisions together. Agreeing on fair contributions of each partner. Making sure both partners have equal access to money. Both benefit equally from financial arrangements.	P A R T N E R S H I P	**TRUST AND SUPPORT** Supporting one another's healthy goals in life. Respecting their right to their own feelings, ideas, friends, activities, opinions, and decisions. Encouraging each other to learn and grow.
SHARED RESPONSIBILITY Mutually agreeing on a fair distribution of work in the home. Making family decisions together.		**RESPECT** Listening to one another non-judgmentally. Being emotionally affirming and understanding. Valuing each other's opinions with honor.
RESPONSIBLE PARENTING Sharing parental responsibilities. Learn healthy parenting by taking classes. Being a positive, nonviolent or non-abusive role model for the children.		**HONESTY & ACCOUNTABILITY** Accepting responsibility for self. Acknowledging past use of unhealthiness and choosing to change. Admitting being wrong. Communicating openly and truthfully. Sharing plans to be healthy in every way with accountability.
GOD AND CHRIST-CENTERED Individually and together, they put God first. They foster and grow in their personal relationship with Jesus daily. They pray together and also keep learning about God, Jesus, and the Holy Spirit.		**ASK FOR HELP** Each person is willing to seek help from a professional, individually or as a couple, when needed. Their goal is to be individually healthy so they can make their marriage healthy.

In a healthy, Christ-centered, loving partnership marriage, there won't be the *continual* use of unhealthy or toxic-abusive words or behaviors. Faith leaders can help couples in healthy and slightly unhealthy Christian marriages by teaching BOTH spouses Christ's healthy characteristics and love standards in classes, workshops, and marriage retreats. When Christian couples learn to live in Christ's love design as equal partners, their marriages will find healing and a new level of love, intimacy, joy, and peace. Healthy marriages following all of the aspects of Christ's love will thrive.

An Unhealthy Marriage

Webster defines unhealthiness as harmful, detrimental, destructive, and damaging to a healthy mind, body, and emotions. At first, we will all have unhealthy elements in our relationships because we all begin our relationships with our imperfect love designs.

I believe many Christian couples struggle because they don't realize they are operating from the unhealthy behaviors they learned in their imperfect definitions of love. They want to have happy marriages, but they just can't stop arguing or occasionally being disrespectful. They are in a tug-of-wills battle. They live in the apostle Paul's statement regarding the struggle with the flesh, "I don't really understand myself, for I want to do what is right, but I don't do it. Instead, I do what I hate." (Rom. 7:15, NLT)

Believers will continue operating from their imperfect love designs by default until they learn and operate in Christ's love. Subconsciously, believers have deemed some unhealthy words and behaviors normal or acceptable, without even knowing it, as long as they or their spouse apologize. Let's look at some examples.

☑ If a believer grows up in a home where their mom is disrespected or degraded by their dad, but he eventually apologizes, they may believe this is how a "normal" and loving marriage should be

☑ If their mom speaks up and their dad tells her that "a good Christian wife" is quiet and submissive, they may believe a wife doesn't have the right to have an opinion, a vote, or say anything to their husband, let alone protest against any abuse

☑ If they heard these statements growing up, "I'm criticizing you because I love you. You always make a big deal out of nothing. I was only joking, so quit being so sensitive," believers equate love as critical and demeaning. They learned that love means your feelings are discounted, and it's all your fault. In other words, the unhealthy or abusive person blames the victim for making them say something mean

☑ The world normalizes bullying by trying to make mean people funny or popular. It also normalizes degrading, disrespect, rape, and all types of abuse in all forms of media. The sensationalizing and rationalizing of sinful behaviors compound the acceptance of unhealthiness and toxic abuse

For decades, Christians have been walking around blind to the fact that they've been operating in imperfect definitions and understandings of love. All the unhealthy and toxic words and actions they have used have been passed down through each generation. We pray for something different, but we are not learning or living God's truth.

Struggling Christians who have come to me for help with their marriages are frustrated, confused, and discouraged because they know something is wrong. No matter how much they pray or try to do the right thing, they continue to struggle. They don't understand that they are repeating unhealthy patterns because they don't know what they don't know. They can only do what they know, and the unhealthiness and toxic abuse continues to be passed on to their children.

Any unhealthy attitudes, words, or behaviors will spill into all our relationships by default. There will be more unhealthy and toxic characteristics in unhealthy marriages. We must also be taught how to guard against letting unhealthiness invade our marriage from becoming inattentive to our spouse. We must do all we can to keep growing our love and marriage centered in Christ.

Until Christ's disciples learn that they have another option, they will continue to live in unhealthy relationships and marriages. If unhealthiness is not identified and corrected with Christ's love standards and the help of professionals over time, it will escalate into a toxic-abusive marriage. The unhealthy person has to be as committed to learning and living healthy behaviors and being held accountable as any person intentional about overcoming any stronghold.

There is a thin line between an unhealthy and toxic-abusive marriage. One unhealthy incident does not make the marriage abusive. However, more than two unhealthy or overtly abusive behaviors in a month or less must raise a red flag.

If there are more than two incidents and the frequency has become more frequent, then in that case, the marriage is on the abusive side, and the victim needs professional help from a counselor experienced in abuse. We must overprotect the victim and remember that she will only tell you the tip of the iceberg. You will learn comments and keywords that victims use in the victim section. Take a few minutes and review the chart for more clarity on what is healthy, unhealthy, and toxic-abusive.

Now, let's look at how destructive a toxic-abusive dictatorship marriage can evolve.

A Toxic-Abusive Dictatorship Marriage

Let's look at an alarming excerpt by Tom Hancock, ABC News:

> Overall, we heard repeatedly from counselors and psychologists that Christian women are less likely to leave abusive marriages, more likely to blame themselves for abuse, more prone to believe the abuse will change, and unlikely to be protected by their pastors.
>
> We found many women felt forced to leave a church when they left a relationship; that they felt forced to choose between faith and safety, and their faith was severely challenged as a result.
>
> On the day we published our first story, Twitter and Facebook lit up: the piece would be read by nearly half a million people. On the second day, at least the same number watched the TV report on 7.30.
>
> On the third day, I received death threats.
>
> ***
>
> The first publication, The Pastoral Report to the Churches on Sexual Violence Against Women and Children in the Church Community, was produced in 1990 in collaboration with the Catholic Church, Anglican Church, Churches of Christ, Uniting Church, and the Salvation Army.
>
> For many women who sought help from a faith leader, it reported, "the response was inadequate ... some faith leaders were uninformed and ill-equipped to

respond to such disclosures, often the advice given wasn't helpful because the faith leader didn't know what kind of advice to give".

One woman told the Victorian royal commission that she had sought help from five different ministers and that each of them had told her to stay with a violent husband. One counselor said, "Be gentle with him, he's trying to be a man."

Another reported telling her pastor that her husband was raping, hitting, and verbally abusing her, while taking drugs. The pastor told her to pray. She then asked him, "What if he kills me first?" And the pastor said: "At least you'll go to heaven."[6]

Allowing the sin and evil of abuse to flourish among God's people is not following God or His healthy marriage design. God's children can no longer ignore the unhealthy and toxic-abusive marriages that are in the church if we are truly following God. We must face facts, learn about abuse, and equip ourselves to teach everyone all the elements of Christ's love and how to live in it to end unhealthy and toxic-abusive marriages among Christ's disciples. Not doing anything is helping the enemy succeed.

"All that is necessary for the triumph of evil is that good men do nothing."

- Edmund Burke

---

6. ABC News: Tom Hancock https://www.abc.net.au/news/2018-05-23/when-women-are-believed-the-church-will-change/9782184 Domestic violence in the church: When women are believed, change will happen. By Julia Baird, posted Tue 22 May 2018 at 1:15 pm, updated Tue 22 May 2018 at 5:22pm.

SNAPSHOT OF A HEALTHY, UNHEALTHY, AND TOXIC ABUSIVE MARRIAGE

MARRIAGE TYPE	CHARACTERISTICS	CHALLENGES
HEALTHY CHRISTIAN MARRIAGE IS A EQUAL, LOVING PARTNERSHIP	• Both spouses keep Christ first in the marriage. • Primarily healthy Christ-like characteristics of the fruits of the Holy Spirit. • BOTH spouses take responsibility for their own stuff and work with Jesus to fix it. • Both spouses will do whatever is necessary to work through any issues in Christ's love and respect.	• Occasional unhealthy behavior may show up 1-2 times a year. • Both spouses are committed to sacrifice and work through any issues: money, children, illness, retirement, etc. • Both spouses will work individually or together with a counselor until the issues are resolved.
	**MOST MARRIAGES OCCASIONALLY STRUGGLE WITH AN UNHEALTHY CHARACTERISTIC OR LIFE ISSUE**	
UNHEALTHY CHRISTIAN MARRIAGE IS A STRUGGLE BETWEEN LIVING IN AN EQUAL LOVING PARTNERSHIP OR A DICTATORSHIP	• Primarily using unhealthy characteristics from their imperfect definitions and understanding of pure love. • They are not committed and engaged in developing their personal relationship with Jesus every day. • They want a happy marriage but don't know how to change things. • As believers, they're confused, frustrated and disappointed with faith, themselves, and each other.	• If they don't learn how to live in Christ's healthy love they will continue being unhealthy. • They may not know their Christ-identity or other discipleship fundamentals. • The dynamics for a toxic abusive marriage is present and must be addressed. • If toxic abusive behaviors remain, there will be abuse.
	**THERE IS A THIN LINE BETWEEN AN UNHEALTHY OR TOXIC-ABUSIVE MARRIAGE (More than two incidents in a month or less must be treated as an abusive marriage**	
TOXIC-ABUSIVE MARRIACE IS A DICTATORSHIP AND THE ABUSER'S CHOICE TO LIVE IN PERPETUAL SIN	• An abuser doesn't have an illness or condition. Abuse is a learned behavior and a choice. An abuser is a Narcissist (self-focused). • The abuser chooses to live in perpetual sin by controlling his spouse with manipulation, coercion, fear, and other destructive tactics to maintain power and control. • Abuse is a sin against God, marriage, and their spouse. • The victim is NEVER the cause or responsible for the abuser's choice to sin.	• A toxic-abusive dictatorship marriage must not be treated like an equal, loving partnership marriage. • The abuser is like a husband who chooses to spray lighter fluid all over his house, spouse, and children. He uses the poison of abuse to control and when that doesn't work. he lights the house on fire to regain control. He doesn't care what it costs the victims. • The victims need our help in a way that keeps her and her children safe.

THE PRIMARY FOCUS MUST BE ON HELPING AND SUPPORTING THE VICTIM
www.GodsTransformingGrace.com

Toxic-Abusive Dictatorship Marriage

This picture of a burning house with the mom and child inside, while the abuser who lit the fire is being helped, is the reality of a toxic-abusive dictatorship marriage. To gain a deeper understanding of a toxic-abusive dictatorship marriage, let's look at the definition and characteristics of a dictatorship.

Webster defines a dictatorship as an absolute undemocratic rule, absolute expression of power in a cruel way, tyranny, ultimate authority, absolutism, oppression, suppression, repression, subjugation, and domination.

These characteristics also follow the definition of a toxic-abusive marriage: unsafe, destructive, damaging, poisonous, dangerous, harmful, malignant, abusive, and possibly deadly.

The abuser does not have an illness or a mental condition. Abuse is a learned behavior and ALWAYS a choice. Abuse is the choice to perpetually sin against God, Jesus, their marriage, spouse, and children.

Historically, Christians and faith leaders have viewed, believed, assumed, and are taught that all marriages are loving equal partnerships. Many faith leaders have never been taught the differences between a healthy, loving partnership marriage and an unhealthy, toxic-abusive marriage. Not knowing the difference between these two types of marriages has placed them and the believers coming to them for help at a dangerous and possibly deadly disadvantage.

A faith leader's unawareness and false perception that all marriages are loving partnerships lead them to believe that any issue in a marriage is automatically a "couples problem." Thinking any marriage issue is a "couples" issue makes both parties responsible for causing the problem, and therefore, both must be part of the solution. However, this belief and understanding are false because one spouse is not responsible for the choice of the other spouse to sin. "So then each of us shall give an account of himself to God." (Rom. 14:12, NIV)

All Marriage Issues are not a "Couples Problem"

One Spouse Choosing to sin

One Spouse Inflicted by Their Spouse's Sin

The victim is not causing the spouse to sin. Therefore, they have no responsibility or power to fix the marriage issue.

Some individual sins that significantly affect a marriage include pornography, lies, adultery, drug or alcohol abuse, addictions, or other individual sins. The spouse choosing the sin or addiction is the only one who can change it. Viewing a toxic-abusive dictatorship marriage as a healthy, loving, equal partnership marriage is false because only the abusive spouse chooses to perpetually sin and devastate the marriage.

Abusers are narcissists and self-serving at any cost. Abuse is a choice. Abusers and victims can be male or female, Christians or nonbelievers. Abuse is not love or God's design for relationships or marriages.

As long as the victim does what her abusive spouse wants, when he wants, and how he wants, she *might* have a good hour or day. Toxic abuse has no place in the life of a disciple of Christ.

There is no way for a disciple of Christ to live in the pure love of God and Jesus and choose to perpetually sin using toxic abuse, destroying the ones they proclaim to love and cherish.

How Believers Are Deceived

Many believers are deceived into an abusive marriage because toxic-abusive people take the time to listen to their hearts. They meet the struggling believers' need to be seen, heard, valued, and belong. The toxic people offer to walk with them on their journeys and deceives them with false hope. They are deceived because they do not know God's truth, power, or the elements of His love.

When believers don't know about Christ's love design or the types and signs of abuse, they don't have a clue that toxic abusers are looking for unaware and unprepared victims to manipulate and control. Victims can't comprehend that their Christian spouses would choose to use toxic-abusive "love" to exert their desire to feel and maintain power and control.

Faith leaders must never forget the motive and goal of abusers is to stay in power and control, no matter what it costs the victims or even themselves. Abusers are perpetually choosing to sin. They are not victims. All faith leaders must understand that a healthy, loving partnership marriage is the opposite of a toxic-abusive dictatorship marriage.

For centuries, the church has focused on the abuser, thinking that the marriage will be fixed if they help him see God's ways. The church has placed saving the marriage over the lives of the victims. Focusing on the abuser is like that fireman going to the abuser's family home that is burning, placing an arm around the abuser who lit the fire, and ignoring the victims still burning inside.

PART 2

ALL ABOUT ABUSE AND THE VICTIM

All About Abuse

What Are the Realities of Abuse?

☑ 48.4% of women and 48.8% of men have experienced at least one psychologically aggressive behavior by an intimate partner[7]

☑ 4 in 10 women and 4 in 10 men have experienced at least one form of coercive control by an intimate partner in their lifetimes[8]

☑ 17.9% of women have experienced a situation where an intimate partner tried to keep them from seeing family and friends[9]

☑ 18.7% of women have experienced threats of physical harm by an intimate partner[10]

☑ 95% of men who physically abuse their intimate partners also psychologically abuse them[11]

☑ Women who earn 65% or more of their households' income are more likely to be psychologically abused than women who earn less than 65% of their households' income[12]

7. Breiding, M. J., Chen, J. & Black, M. C. (2014). Intimate partner violence in the United States – 2010. Retrieved from http://www.cdc.gov/violenceprevention/pdf/ cdc_nisvs_ipv_report_2013_v17_single_a.pdf.

8. Breiding, M. J., Chen, J. & Black, M. C. (2014). Intimate partner violence in the United States – 2010. Retrieved from http://www.cdc.gov/violenceprevention/pdf/ cdc_nisvs_ipv_report_2013_v17_single_a.pdf.

9. Breiding, M. J., Chen, J. & Black, M. C. (2014). Intimate partner violence in the United States – 2010. Retrieved from http://www.cdc.gov/violenceprevention/pdf/ cdc_nisvs_ipv_report_2013_v17_single_a.pdf.

10. Breiding, M. J., Chen, J. & Black, M. C. (2014). Intimate partner violence in the United States – 2010. Retrieved from http://www.cdc.gov/violenceprevention/pdf/ cdc_nisvs_ipv_report_2013_v17_single_a.pdf.

11. Henning, K., & Klesges, L.M (2003). Prevalence and characteristics of psychological abuse reported by court-involved battered women. Journal of Interpersonal Violence, 18(8), 857-871.

12. Kaukinen, C. (2004). Status compatibility, physical violence, and emotional abuse in intimate relationships. Journal of Marriage and Family, 66(2), 452-471.

What Happens to the Children in the Cycle of Abuse?

☑ More than 3 million children witness acts of domestic violence every year in their homes: the place they should be the safest. In homes where there is domestic violence, the children are abused at a rate 1500% higher than the national average[13]

☑ Little boys who grow up in homes where domestic violence is occurring are 100 times more likely to become abusers than boys in violence-free homes[14]

☑ 81% of men who batter had fathers who abused their mothers[15]

These facts are equally true for Christians and non-believers. There is no difference in the numbers, and these facts should set all of Christ's disciples on high alert!

In Part 1, you learned that it is harder for a Christian woman to tell anyone about the abuse because she is not believed, and the church has prioritized keeping a marriage intact over the safety and life of a victim. Remember the woman who went to her pastor for help in Tom Hancock's report for ABC News.

> She told the pastor that her husband was raping, hitting, and verbally abusing her, while taking drugs. The pastor told her to pray. She then asked him, "What if he kills me first?" And the pastor said: "At least you'll go to heaven."[16]

Allowing the sin and evil of abuse to flourish among God's people is not following God. God's children can no longer ignore the unhealthy and toxic-abusive marriages that are in any church family if they are truly following God.

We must face facts, learn about abuse, and equip ourselves to teach everyone all the elements of Christ's love and how to live in it to end unhealthy and toxic-abusive marriages among Christ's church. Not doing anything is helping the enemy succeed.

13. National Coalition Against Domestic Violence, Washington D.C. National Coalition Against Domestic Violence (NCADV). https://ncadv.org/STATISTICS

14. Senator Joseph Biden, Violence Against Women: Victims of the System (Washington D.C.: U.S. Senate Committee on the Judiciary

15. "The Effects of Domestic Violence on Children", N.J. Department of Community of Community Affairs, Division of Women

16. ABC News: Tom Hancock   https://www.abc.net.au/news/2018-05-23/when-women-are-believed-the-church-will-change/9782184 Domestic violence in the church: When women are believed, change will happen. By Julia Baird, posted Tue 22 May 2018 at 1:15 pm, updated Tue 22 May 2018 at 5:22pm.

What Is Abuse?

Remember, we're using the woman as the victim because of the statistics that show the majority of victims are women. We acknowledge men are also abused.

Abuse is words, actions, or a combination used intentionally to hold power and control over another person through manipulation, intimidation, threats, physical force, and any other form of abuse. Abuse is not an illness or condition. Abuse is a learned behavior and a choice to perpetually sin.

Many people, including abused victims, believe that unless a woman has a black eye or a broken bone, she is not being abused. There are testimonies of thousands of women sharing the physical, emotional, and psychological wounds of abuse that no one sees.

Dr. Walker LE, a psychologist and expert on domestic violence, and Huss MT., a forensic psychologist, share their summary of how the cycle of domestic abuse is played out in a relationship.

> Abuse is rarely constant but alternates between four stages: period of tension building (tension starts and steadily builds, abuser starts to get angry, communication breaks down, victim feels the need to concede to the abuser, tension becomes too much, victim feels uneasy); acting out period (any type of abuse occurs); the honeymoon period (abuser apologizes for abuse, some beg forgiveness or show sorrows, abuser may promise it will never happen again, blames victim for provoking the abuse or denies abuse occurred, minimizing); the calm period (abuse stops, abuser acts like the abuse never happened, promises made during honeymoon stage may be met, abuser may give gifts to victim, victim believes or wants to believe that the abuse is over or that the abuser will change).[17]

To help faith leaders understand this process, let's learn the top eight types of abuse and signs in a toxic-abusive marriage.

---

17. https://www.ncbi.nlm.nih.gov/pmc/articles/PMC4768593/, Health Psychol Res. 2014 Nov 6; 2(3): 1821. Published online 2014 Oct 22. doi: 10.4081/hpr.2014.1821, PMCID: PMC4768593, PMID: 26973948, Domestic Violence and Abuse in Intimate Relationship from Public Health Perspective, author Zlatka Rakovec-Felser.

Top Eight Types and Signs of Abuse

The laws and police responses to abuse reports vary from state to state. Not all abuse is against the law, like emotional, financial, and some verbal abuse. Some laws are changing, like bullying being addressed as verbal and psychological abuse.

However, in every state, it is illegal to inflict physical threats, bodily harm, stalking, and rape within or outside of marriage. Let's look at the top eight types and signs of abuse. Note that many of the signs and types overlap.

1. **Physical Abuse:** Physical abuse is any deliberate act of force against a person that results in physical harm, injury, or trauma. Physical abuse includes hitting, kicking, burning, cutting, scalding, biting, or pushing. It also includes the misuse of medication, forced feeding or withholding of food, and incorrect use of restrictive practices – where there is unauthorized use of restraint against an individual or unwarranted confinement

2. **Sexual Abuse:** Sexual abuse occurs when an individual is forced, pressured, or tricked into taking part in sexual activity with another person, persons, object, or animal. The person may have expressed that they didn't want to be involved, may not be able to give consent (drunk or drugged), or may not have the capacity to understand what is happening (which includes special needs people). Sexual abuse includes rape, indecent exposure, inappropriate looking or touching, sexual harassment, teasing or innuendo, sexual photography or subjection to pornography, witnessing sexual acts they did not consent to or were pressured into, or their partner regulates their access to birth control. Refusing sex because the abuser deems their partner ugly, fat, etc., is also abuse

3. **Verbal Abuse:** In verbal abuse, the abuser attacks the victim with overt forms of abuse like name-calling, threats, constantly correcting, interrupting, putting down, humiliating, and demeaning them. Even prolonged silent treatment is a form of verbal abuse

4. **Emotional and Psychological Abuse:** Psychological (also referred to as emotional) abuse is any type of behavior involving emotional mistreatment of a person. It includes threats of harm or abandonment to the victim or the children, enforced social isolation (such as preventing the victim from seeing family or accessing external services, like education), not respecting privacy or boundaries, intimidating, coercing, or threatening someone, cyber-bullying, or preventing someone from meeting their religious and cultural needs, their expression of choice and opinion, or meaningful activities and stimulation. One

frequent ploy of the abuser is to accuse and harass the victim about imagined affairs or other false claims

5. **Gaslighting:** Gaslighting uses more insidious mind games like making the victim question their judgments, reality, or sanity by moving, hiding, and changing things, or pretending things didn't happen the way the victim remembers

6. **Financial Abuse***:* Financial or material abuse involves the abuser using or misusing money to control the victim's actions and freedom and using their funds or belongings without their permission. Types of financial abuse include scams (both online and in-person), theft, fraud, coercion to file false tax records, coercion for their financial affairs or arrangements such as their will, property, business, or inheritance, the misuse or misappropriation of property, possessions or benefits. Financial abuse also covers preventing or controlling the ability of the victim to work, demanding they stay at home, control of all money even if the victim is working, having all credit cards and bank accounts in the abuser's name and control, and leaving the victim no access to money or having to beg for money

7. **Neglect and Abandonment:** Neglect includes the failure to provide adequate food, clothing, shelter, medical treatment, or financial support. Abandonment includes being left without the resources or ability to obtain necessary food, clothing, shelter, health care, and money. It also includes mental, emotional, psychological, or physical abandonment by a spouse or partner and the irresponsibility of the abuser to earn money or squandering it away

8. **Spiritual Abuse:** Spiritual abuse occurs when an oppressor (the abuser or a faith leader) establishes control and domination by using scripture, blame, guilt, shame, doctrine, or his "leadership role or position" as a weapon to keep the victim quiet and in the abusive marriage. Spiritual abusers can be Pastors, Christians, husbands, or any other person in a leadership role. Spiritual abuse can be subtle because it can mask itself as a religious practice when a husband exhibits control-oriented leadership over his wife. He lords his power over her, demands submission from her, even though he disrespects and abuses her, or he uses scripture in shaming and punishing ways; he is abusing her

Darby Strickland, with Focus on the Family, speaks out against spiritual abuse.

When a spiritual abuser twists scripture and uses it to attack, his abuse can feel as though it comes from God himself. Even though the abuser is taking scripture out of context, distorting it and weaponizing it, the oppressor is using God's words — so it can seem as if God is the one doing the shaming.

Spiritual abuse is a close cousin to emotional abuse, except it's more profoundly wounding as it often leaves victims isolated from God. Since it uses God and His Word to dominate and scold, victims can find it hard to separate the abuse from their understanding of who God is or of how He sees them.[18]

In my first abusive marriage, I went to three pastors for help. All three told me to submit to my husband because marriage is Holy, forgive and forget or God would not forgive me, and stay in my marriage because God hates divorce. These three spiritually abusive pastors were instrumental in my choice to stay for thirteen years in my first abusive marriage. As a result, all of the abuse my two sons and I endured almost ended in homicide because I couldn't see another way out.

Fast forward twenty years, and I see the turmoil my boys are in because of the abuse we all endured from their dad and what they heard from the pulpit. They struggle with pain, addictions, fear, and believing God is good. Although I share how much God has healed me, they still struggle to trust anyone from a church.

I have told them that people got things wrong but not God. God NEVER condones any type of abuse in any relationship or marriage. Abuse is not God's will, and faith leaders must now work on ways to educate believers to stop perpetuating this pandemic.

Steps to End Spiritual Abuse

The first step to ending spiritual abuse is to acknowledge it exists. Next, we must teach all faith leaders about spiritual abuse and how to prevent it. Faith leaders have to be willing to examine and change the unbiblical, spiritually abusive scriptures used out of context and even the practices the church has deemed Biblical concerning unhealthy and toxic abusive marriages. All words and actions must follow God's word and Christ's loving standards of respect, responsibility, and accountability, including no manipulation or holding power or control over others.

Christ's disciples must listen, help, and support victims over abusers, no matter how bad it looks for the church. We must value victims and their safety over keeping a toxic-abusive marriage together or keeping it quiet. To end spiritual abuse, we must be part of the solution.

---

18. https://www.focusonthefamily.com/marriage/what-is-spiritual-abuse-in-marriage/ What is Spiritual Abuse in Marriage? By Darby Strickland, September 13, 2021.

Cycle of Abuse

One evening on a camping trip, my friend and I went fishing with my dad. My dad caught a giant catfish and reeled it in. My friend had never caught a fish, so my dad decided to let the fish swim back out into the lake and let my friend reel it in again. She was so excited, but as the fish got closer to the shore, it stopped fighting. It's like the fish knew it was powerless and just gave up.

The story illustrates the debilitating cycle of abuse and how the abuser uses the power to lure and control a victim through the tactics of fear, manipulation, isolation, coercion, and the false hope of better times.

The victim wants so much to believe that one day God will magically turn her husband into the man she fell in love with if she believes, prays, and stays. But the cycle of abuse will continue until the victim or the abuser chooses to stop the cycle.

When we look at God's design for marriage, all the aspects of Christ's love, how God's word instructs us to love others as Jesus loved us, and the fruits of the Spirit, there is no way to rationalize or justify any form of abuse. The next step to understanding unhealthiness and toxic abuse is to look at how the abuser uses one or more tactics from the Cycle of Abuse Wheel to establish and maintain control over his spouse.

Abusers will always use a continually changing combination of tactics to keep the victims focused on trying to fix everything or to avoid "setting off" the abusers. As the victims focus on preventing and surviving the abuse, they don't have time to see or counter the abuse tactics. Let's look at each section.

Note that the abuse cycle differs from the secular abuse wheel for two reasons. This abuse cycle graph has a Spiritual Abuse Tactic and a Loving Husband Deception tactic.

Cycle of Abuse Wheel of Power and Control

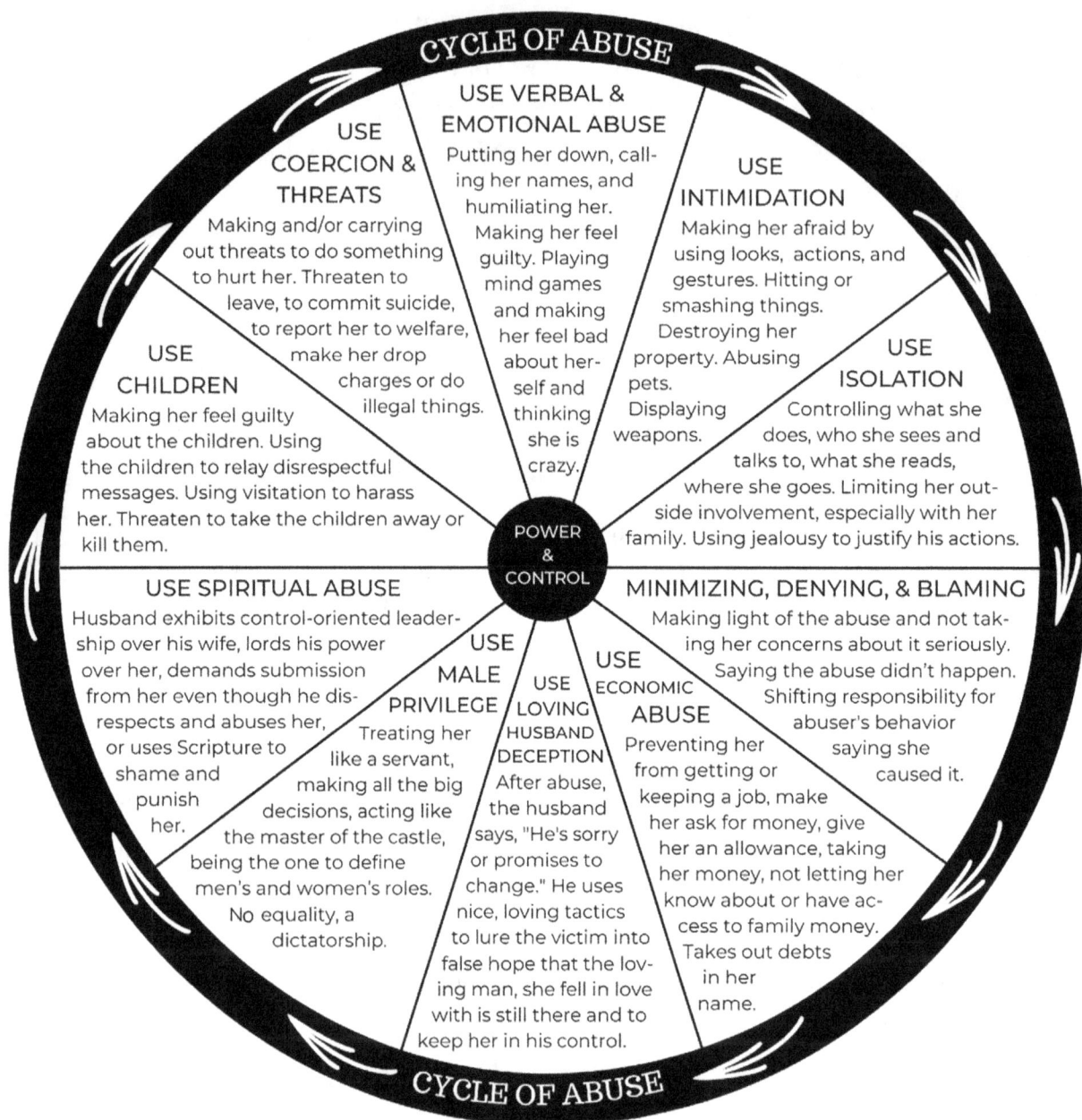

CYCLE OF ABUSE

USE VERBAL & EMOTIONAL ABUSE
Putting her down, calling her names, and humiliating her. Making her feel guilty. Playing mind games and making her feel bad about herself and thinking she is crazy.

USE COERCION & THREATS
Making and/or carrying out threats to do something to hurt her. Threaten to leave, to commit suicide, to report her to welfare, make her drop charges or do illegal things.

USE INTIMIDATION
Making her afraid by using looks, actions, and gestures. Hitting or smashing things. Destroying her property. Abusing pets. Displaying weapons.

USE CHILDREN
Making her feel guilty about the children. Using the children to relay disrespectful messages. Using visitation to harass her. Threaten to take the children away or kill them.

USE ISOLATION
Controlling what she does, who she sees and talks to, what she reads, where she goes. Limiting her outside involvement, especially with her family. Using jealousy to justify his actions.

POWER & CONTROL

USE SPIRITUAL ABUSE
Husband exhibits control-oriented leadership over his wife, lords his power over her, demands submission from her even though he disrespects and abuses her, or uses Scripture to shame and punish her.

USE MALE PRIVILEGE
Treating her like a servant, making all the big decisions, acting like the master of the castle, being the one to define men's and women's roles. No equality, a dictatorship.

USE LOVING HUSBAND DECEPTION
After abuse, the husband says, "He's sorry or promises to change." He uses nice, loving tactics to lure the victim into false hope that the loving man, she fell in love with is still there and to keep her in his control.

USE ECONOMIC ABUSE
Preventing her from getting or keeping a job, make her ask for money, give her an allowance, taking her money, not letting her know about or have access to family money. Takes out debts in her name.

MINIMIZING, DENYING, & BLAMING
Making light of the abuse and not taking her concerns about it seriously. Saying the abuse didn't happen. Shifting responsibility for abuser's behavior saying she caused it.

CYCLE OF ABUSE

God's Transforming Grace ™

All of these tactics are part of the cycle of abuse that must be understood and stopped. Many abused women describe their spouses as Dr. Jekyll and Mr. Hyde. They believe that the few good times reveal their real husbands. However, they primarily live with the beast personality of their spouses, and that's what gets them confused. It's vital for faith leaders to educate them that this tactic is just a tool in the abusers' mind games and tactics to remain in control over them.

You cannot love like Jesus and use any of these tactics. All abusive tactics go against the two greatest commandments, the character of Jesus Christ, and the equal loving partnership of marriage God designed. According to God's word, when husbands love their wives, none of these mindsets, words, or behaviors can live in His marriage design.

> Husbands, go all out in your love for your wives, exactly as Christ did for the church—a love marked by giving, not getting. Christ's love makes the church whole. His words evoke her beauty. Everything he does and says is designed to bring the best out of her, dressing her in dazzling white silk, radiant with holiness. And that is how husbands ought to love their wives. They're really doing themselves a favor—since they're already "one" in marriage. No one abuses his own body, does he? No, he feeds and pampers it. That's how Christ treats us, the church, since we are part of his body. (Eph. 5:25-30, MSG)

When a wife is loved as if she was Christ in the flesh, which she is because Jesus lives in all his disciples, then it is an honor for a wife to submit to a husband's decision because she knows he serves God first and his decision will honor God and her in every way. There is no place for unhealthiness or toxic abuse in a Christian marriage or any relationship. To help us understand the victim better and how we can help her, let's look at her realities.

"In Her Shoes" Exercise

The "In Her Shoes"[19] exercise is a virtual experiential learning exercise that helps people think and make choices as a victim in her abusive relationship. Each scenario is based on a victim's experiences in real life. They are designed to help participants learn and talk about the many realities a victim must work through to learn, survive, or break free. You will have the opportunity to walk in a survivor's shoes for a short time by reading the options, making choices, and following the directions.

A heads-up: All of the survivors in this activity are women. We know that all genders experience domestic and sexual abuse, and the focus on women in this activity is not meant to minimize or erase the experiences of abused men. Furthermore, the victims in these stories experience some troubling things, and the simulation is incomplete without a follow-up debrief.

Be aware that if you or a loved one has suffered abuse, this exercise may trigger emotions or memories that you will need to address with your counselor. If you need additional support, call 1-800-799-7233 or www.thehotline.org.

Pick at least three women from the eight characters and write your thoughts and questions in the space below. To access the exercise, go to https://bit.ly/36DVP6y.

---

19. https://wscadv.org/training-kits/in-her-shoes/, created by Washington State Coalition Against Domestic Violence.

Character Summary 1:

Options and the impact of people:

Insights:

Character Summary 2:

Options and the impact of people:

Insights:

Character Summary 3:

Options and the impact of people:

Insights:

Why Doesn't She Just Leave?

How many of us struggle with something, whether it be food, exercise, gossiping, lying, addiction, or hidden sin? Why don't we just stop? Whatever we struggle with has layers that we must untangle to get to the core and break free. After doing the exercise "In Her Shoes," you have a better understanding of the complexities a victim of abuse must traverse to find the truth, help, support, resources, and freedom.

Although the victim in a toxic-abusive marriage doesn't cause or force her abusive husband to hurt her, she is burdened with the mental and emotional devastation that can deplete her confidence, hope, and faith. She must also face the limitations her abuser places on her to have support and the ability to work to take care of herself and her children. As a victim searches for answers, what she hears from others can be the difference between finding truth or being inflicted with more judgment, condemnation, shame, guilt, and spiritual abuse.

I know from personal experience how devastating the words of Christians can be to a victim's heart, spirit, mind, and life. I don't believe most Christians intentionally try to hurt victims caught in the cycle of abuse. However, their use of scriptures taken out of context mixed with "Christianese" sayings can be devastating.

Broken people don't need a one-liner that justifies the hard or hurtful things going on in their lives. They need to know how to hold the hand of Jesus and walk through the fire.

Whenever you make a statement without knowing where people are coming from or their knowledge and understanding of God's truth, you can wound them.

Let's look at a few of the damaging or hurtful statements, questions, and verses I heard from Christians, pastors, and other faith leaders after I had shared incidents of abuse.

- ☑ God won't give you more than you can handle

- ☑ If you pray hard enough and have a deeper faith, God will change your husband

- ☑ Be kind, understanding, and submissive to your husband, and God will show him how to be a better spouse

- ☑ Submit to your husband

- ☑ No one is perfect, and sometimes God calls us to endure

- ☑ God hates divorce, so don't use this as an easy way out

- ☑ We all make mistakes. Forgive and forget what your husband has done, or God won't forgive you

- ☑ Why does she stay? If it were me, I would leave. I wouldn't put up with that

- ☑ There must be some reason he is treating her this way

- ☑ She must be stupid and dumb to let someone hurt her

- ☑ She must like to be hurt, or why would she stay?

All of these statements discount and dismiss any abuse the victim has endured. They imply that the victim is causing and deserving of the abuse, or she made it up, or she is blowing the problems out of proportion.

They put no responsibility for the abuse or accountability on the abuser. They also feed into the dictatorship marriage, heaping spiritual abuse on top of the victim's already unbearable load of abuse. These statements place all of the abuser's sins and the responsibility of having a good marriage solely on the victim.

In the exercise "In Her Shoes," you witnessed the impact of people's words on the victim and how they affected her options and choices. After seeing all the complexities and mental anguish a victim must traverse to find the truth, support, and healing to break free, let's look at the definition, types, signs, and cycle of abuse in the next section.

The Victim

Realities of a Victim

The realities of a Christian woman in an abusive marriage vary on her faith beliefs, knowledge, emotional support, financial abilities, and resources. As you learned in the exercise, "In Her Shoes," a victim must unravel her pain from her basic needs just to understand what is happening, let alone break free.

After a victim tries to fix her marriage and find answers without success, she may reach out for help. Depending on her feedback, she can be empowered to keep moving forward and break free or be judged and condemned, feeling like she has no choice but to stay.

Christian women in unhealthy or toxic-abusive dictatorship marriages have five main hurdles to cross. They include unawareness, fear, misinformation, financial reasons, and health. Understanding these main hurdles can help faith leaders meet victims in their confusion and bring clarity. Let's look at these hurdles.

1. **Unawareness:** Victims don't know what they don't know. Victims don't know that they're operating from their imperfect definition of love. They don't know all of the aspects of Christ's healthy love, the differences between healthy, unhealthy, and toxic-abusive relationships, the types and signs of abuse, or what God says about love and marriage.

   Many believers are operating from the misquoted and misused Bible verses they heard referring to love, marriage, forgiveness, reconciliation, and abuse. They don't know abuse is not a condition or illness or that abuse is a learned behavior and a choice an abuser makes to perpetually sin to maintain power and control. They are not taught that abuse is NEVER God's will or acceptable in marriage.

2. **Finances:** Most abuse victims don't have access to finances or the current career skills needed to provide for herself and her children. The National Coalition Against Domestic Violence states that 85% of victims returned to abusive marriages for financial reasons.[20]

   Even if a victim has a career, the abuser takes control of her money. The abuser always focuses on destroying her self-esteem and confidence, so she questions

---

20. National Coalition Against Domestic Violence, Washington D.C. National Coalition Against Domestic Violence (NCADV). https://ncadv.org/STATISTICS

her ability to work. If she has a great job, he threatens to ruin her reputation if she doesn't give him control of her earnings. The abuser leads the victim to believe that she could not make it without him; no one will help her or believe her, so she needs to stay.

3. **Fear:** The abuser constantly uses the threat of hurting her or her children, taking her children away, or killing all of them to keep the victim in line. The abuser continually tells the victim that she is a bad mom and doesn't deserve her children. He also uses one or both of the following tactics to keep her trapped.

He reminds her that he has control of all the money to get the best lawyer, and she has nothing. He also threatens to kill her and the children if she considers leaving. Constantly holding these threats over the victim can keep her paralyzed in fear and protection mode. What would you do to keep your children safe? Here are some statistics about the real threat of death to victims that we must always be cautious of.

- 72% of all murder-suicides involve an intimate partner; 94% of the victims of these murder suicides are female[21]
- The presence of a gun in a domestic violence situation increases the risk of homicide by 500%[22]
- Up to 75% of abused women who are murdered are killed after they leave their partners[23]

The statistics above must keep all faith leaders aware of the life and death risks victims take when they finally find the courage to come forward. Many victims find the courage, only to be disbelieved, dismissed, or told to stay in the toxic-abusive marriages by faith leaders. All of these ungodly, devastating responses directly oppose God's truth and the loving life of Jesus Christ.

Faith leaders must never forget that every decision the victim makes can be the difference between life or death, even in a "Christian" marriage. Let us be the hope of Christ and the truth of God that helps victims untangle from their toxic-abusive marriages and live in Christ's healthy love. Let us be the help of Christ.

4. **Beliefs and Assumptions About Marriage:** In the marriage section, we learned that most Christians enter their marriages believing they are a loving, equal partnership. They believe their spouse has the same or similar definitions of love, marriage, what it means to be a Christian wife or husband, forgiveness,

---

21. https://vpc.org/revealing-the-impacts-of-gun-violence/murder-suicide/

22. https://www.ncbi.nlm.nih.gov/pmc/articles/PMC1447915/ Risk Factors for Femicide in Abusive Relationships: Results From a Multisite Case Control Study, Am J Public Health, 2003 July; 93(7): 1089-1097

23. https://www.theguardian.com/money/us-money-blog/2014/oct/20/domestic-private-violence-women-men-abuse-hbo-ray-rice The Gardian, Interview by Jana Kasperkevic.

reconciliation, trust, freedom, respect, accountability, safe boundaries, or what is healthy, unhealthy, or toxic-abusive.

However, depending on the messages they heard from their parents, other Christians, leadership, and role models, they may not have been taught what healthy, unhealthy, or toxic-abusive love looks like. As believers operate in their imperfect love and unawareness of God's truth, Christ's love, what is healthy, and the types and signs of abuse, they are vulnerable to being abused.

In a Christian marriage, it usually takes the victim years to figure out that their "Christian" marriage is unhealthy or toxic-abusive. Victims do everything and anything to make their marriages work. They want to keep their families together and honor their marriage vows.

They exhaust their minds, emotions, and strength to figure things out on their own. They follow the advice to forgive and try to forget, trust, believe, pray harder, and submit, no matter what the abuser does. They stay in their marriages to try and save their marriages, as instructed, because God hates divorce.

They have believed that being a good "Christian wife" means they are solely responsible for making their marriages work. With all this misinformation and incorrect counsel and guidance from faith leaders and other Christians, the victims struggle to keep from drowning in confusion, uncertainty, helplessness, and hopelessness.

The hurdle of beliefs and assumptions is the largest one for Christian victims to overcome. All of these realities make it crucial for faith leaders to learn how to identify, support, and teach victims about Christ's healthy love and God's truth, so they can work with Jesus and break free.

5. **Health:** The toll of all the mental, verbal, physical, sexual, and other forms of abuse on the victim affects their entire health. Victims suffer from depression, anxiety, stomach problems, insomnia, immune disorders, cancer, and many other symptoms. Not only are they trying to fix their marriages, protect their children and their lives, go to work, and attend Bible studies, but they also have to do it all while suffering many mental and physical afflictions.

   - 1 in 4 victims of abuse attempt suicide[24]
   - Children who grow up in an abusive home commit suicide at twice the national average[25]

24. https://www.sciencedaily.com/releases/2019/01/190109192533.htm, Science News, Child abuse linked to ris of suicide in later life. January 9, 2019, University of Manchester. Journal reference: Ioannis Angelakis, Emma Louise Gillespie, Maria Panagioti. Childhood maltreatment and adult suicidality: a comprehensive systematic review with meta-analysis. Psychological Medicine, 2019; 1 DOI: 10.1017/S0033291718003823

25. http://www.suicide.org/domestic-violence-and-suicide.html, Suicide.org, Domestic Violence and Suicide.

Untangling from a toxic-abusive marriage is an excruciating process that takes time. Unfortunately, when a victim is a believer, the extra layer of confusion about healthy love, marriage, and what God's will is can be difficult. The best way faith leaders can help victims is to teach them to study God's word and learn His truth for themselves.

Mindsets of a Victim

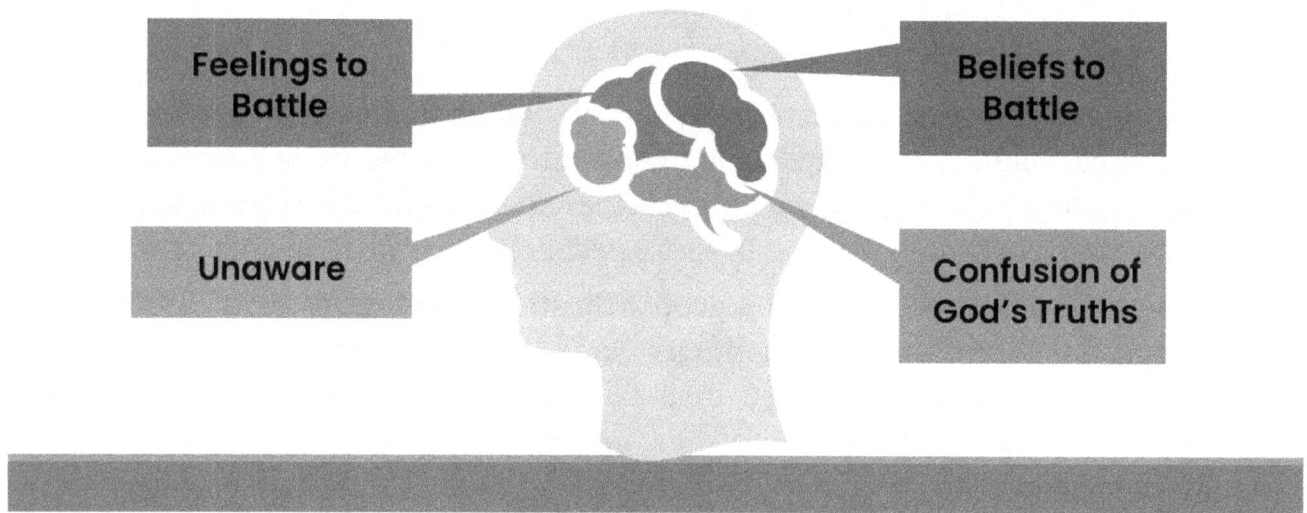

As the victim begins to realize the unhealthiness or toxic abuse in her marriage, she must fight the battle first in her mind. Once she learns God's truth and the elements of Christ's love, she will know how to take her thoughts captive and take control of her feelings. Let's look at the following list to help us see some of the top mind-battles victims must overcome in four main categories.

Top Mind Battles for Victims

Unaware

☑ She doesn't know she's operating in her imperfect definition of love or that she can change it

☑ She doesn't know Christ's love or design

☑ She doesn't know what's healthy or the types and signs of abuse

☑ She doesn't know abuse is a learned behavior and the abuser's choice to perpetually sin

Feelings to Battle

☑ Fear of safety and loss of life

☑ She feels shame and false guilt for allowing the abuse to happen

☑ She is afraid of what other people will think and say

☑ She's afraid of rejection and abandonment from friends, family, or the church

☑ She is afraid of her abuser's punishment if she speaks up

Beliefs to Battle

☑ She believes she's stupid or deserves abuse

☑ She blames herself for causing the abuse

☑ She believes she's alone

☑ No one will believe or help her

☑ She has no power

Confusion of God's Truths

☑ Her prayers, sacrifice, and staying in her marriage will heal her abusive spouse

☑ She believes the misquoted and misused scripture because she doesn't know God's word herself

☑ Believes all Christian marriages are equal partnerships and it will work out

☑ She doesn't know unhealthiness and abuse are not God's will for her marriage

☑ She doesn't understand God's marriage design as a healthy, equal partnership

☑ She doesn't know her value in Christ

☑ She has been misinformed that all things in marriage are Holy and that if she suffers, it is God's will

A victim is overwhelmed with the battles in her mind and emotions while trying to survive all the pain from her toxic-abusive husband. When she finally builds up the courage to ask a faith leader for help, the last thing a victim needs is to be dismissed or endure spiritual abuse from them.

Faith Leader's Statements That Can Harm Victims

Many faith leaders have avoided helping victims because they do not want to make things worse by saying the wrong things or inflicting spiritual abuse. Remember, spiritual abuse occurs when an oppressor (the abuser or a faith leader) establishes control and domination by using scripture, doctrine, or his "leadership role" as a weapon to keep the victim quiet or in the abusive marriage.

As a faith leader, you must not treat all marriages as loving partnerships, or you risk heaping spiritual abuse on the victim. Remember, abusive marriages are dictatorships. Be mindful of the verses you choose to encourage a believer in their walk with Jesus or their marriage. Unless you know the person coming to you for help is in a healthy, loving partnership marriage, lean to the side of them being a victim to avoid any spiritual abuse.

Some of these statements and verses have truth and can be used to help each spouse grow in a healthy, equal partnership marriage. However, these statements confuse and blame the victim in a toxic-abusive dictatorship marriage.

Statements and verses that help spouses in an equal partnership marriage work the opposite way in a toxic-abusive dictatorship marriage. Asking an abusive spouse for equality or sharing of opinions only escalates more abuse. Following unrealistic statements of what it takes to have a "happy, healthy marriage" in a toxic-abusive dictatorship marriage makes victims question their faith and what is wrong with them because the abuse increases.

When you are a victim, any statement implying you caused the abuse you are enduring or that you have the power to change it is not true. The victims are not choosing to sin. Therefore, they do not have the power to change the abusers.

Let's look at some of the statements faith leaders use that can harm victims, even though there may be a piece of truth.

☑Every couple has marriage problems, and it takes two to make them and fix them

☑All marriage problems can be overcome through Christ; you must remain faithful

☑Never forget God put man as the head, authority, and rulership over the marriage

☑ Godly wives are quiet and submit to their husbands in every way

☑ Whatever goes on in your Christian home is Holy and your business, not church business

☑ You must be more understanding and "Forgive your husband or God will not forgive you." (Matt. 6:14, NIV) Remember that you are not perfect either

☑ Husbands deserve more understanding, as they are the primary breadwinner

☑ You owe your husband loyalty and respect, so never cross these lines

☑ God will never give you more than you can handle

☑ Christians don't have abusive marriages

☑ Rape is not possible in a Holy Christian marriage because the "marriage bed is undefiled"

☑ "Love keeps no record of wrongs." (1 Cor. 13:1, NIV) True forgiveness means you don't hold on and remember anything in the past

Here are several verses on suffering that are also misused and quoted to victims to justify or rationalize their abuse as Godly suffering. Misusing these verses twists the Bible into a weapon that brings the victims confusion, pain, helplessness, and hopelessness.

☑ But even if you should suffer for what is right, you are blessed. "Do not fear their threats; do not be frightened" (1 Peter 3:14, NIV)

☑ Therefore, since Christ suffered in his body, arm yourselves also with the same attitude, because whoever suffers in the body is done with sin (1 Peter 4:1, NIV)

☑ More than that, we rejoice in our sufferings, knowing that suffering produces endurance, and endurance produces character, and character produces hope, and hope does not put us to shame, because God's love has been poured into our hearts through the Holy Spirit who has been given to us (Rom. 5:3-5. ESV)

☑ He was despised and rejected by mankind, a man of suffering, and familiar with pain. Like one from whom people hide their faces he was despised, and we held him in low esteem (Isa. 53:3. NIV)

Many faith leaders do not realize they are inflicting spiritual abuse because they have not learned about the types and signs of abuse; therefore, they treat all marriages as an equal loving partnership. Unfortunately, I have heard most of the previous misused statements and scriptures from faith leaders to avoid them from getting involved, to keep me silent, and to stay in my toxic-abusive marriage.

If unhealthiness or toxic abuse is never acknowledged, many faith leaders believe they can avoid dealing with it. However, turning a blind eye, dismissing unhealthiness or toxic abuse as a marriage problem, excusing any unhealthy or abusive behavior, or blaming the victims directly opposes God's truth and Christ's love.

Never forget that spiritual abuse is about control through scripture, position, and acting as God's ultimate knowledge and authority, regardless of the cost to the individual or her children. God placed the husband as the spiritual head of the marriage, and he is also considered an overseer. In these roles, let's see what God says.

> Now the overseer is to be above reproach, faithful to his wife, temperate, self-controlled, respectable, hospitable, able to teach, not given to drunkenness, not violent but gentle, not quarrelsome, not a lover of money. (1 Tim. 3:2-3, NIV)

> If anyone, then, knows the good they ought to do and doesn't do it, it is sin for them. (James 4:17, NIV)

Meeting Victims Where They Are in Nine Absolute Truths

You have learned about the complexities a victim must face before she even comes to a faith leader for help. You have also learned how victims have been hurt and condemned by faith leaders. Now we will discuss what is necessary for a victim to feel safe, heard, and hopeful for her future.

Faith leaders will need to set up key people to meet with victims, preferably victims that have healed and are healthy. These advocates will need to go through this education and also use the following list of truths and the ten guidelines to help them be prepared. Faith leaders can no longer be unequipped and unprepared if they are going to be part of the solution to end the pandemic of unhealthy and toxic-abusive marriages in the body of Christ's church. Let's look at these absolute truths.

Nine Absolute Truths When You Meet with a Victim

To meet victims where they are, faith leaders must communicate these truths in Christ's love and compassion.

1. Abuse is not an illness, condition, or anger issue. It is a learned behavior and a choice to perpetually sin made solely by the abuser

2. She has never said or done anything deserving of any type of abuse

3. Abuse is wrong and a sin against her, God, and Jesus Christ living in her

4. Abuse is not God's punishment for her sins nor God's will in any relationship or marriage

5. God has not abandoned her, and He promises to help her (Matt. 28:20, NIV)

6. Assure her that her angry feelings are normal, especially since she has been hurt. Encourage her to hold Christ's hand and seek professional help to guard against letting her anger get out of control

7. Remind her that God made us for relationships and community and the abusive isolation tactic directly opposes God's word

8. Don't talk about forgiving the abuser at this point. If she asks, tell her forgiveness comes in layers. Forgiveness doesn't mean you ignore or forget the abuse, become a doormat, or that you have to trust your spouse or stay in an unhealthy or toxic-abusive marriage

9. Encourage her to talk with a counselor experienced with abuse to help her get clear on her thoughts and emotions and make a safety plan if things get too dangerous

Communicating these truths helps victims know that you hear them and believe them. It has taken them years and all their courage and strength to share anything with you. They are taking one of the biggest risks in their lives, and faith leaders must honor and guard their vulnerability. To help you in your meeting, follow the twelve guidelines below.

Meeting with Victims Guidelines

1. **Always Pray First:** Pray for God to help you discern what the believer needs and how He can use you as His vessel of truth and love

2. **Safety First Is the Faith Leader's Top Priority:** A faith leader's top priority and concern must always be for the safety of the victim and her children
   - Provide a safe place to meet and allow 1 – 1 1/2 hours
   - Provide confidentiality and confidence that you will only talk with her

- Let her know that she will have to contact you to set up meetings to keep her safe. You won't call, text, or email and put her in danger if her spouse sees them

- Ask her if she feels safe at home. If she says no, ask her if you can call the local safe house so she can talk with a professional right away to see what is best to do. If you need to call the police, do so and wait with her until they come

- The victim must make her choice and take action when she is ready. Never act on her behalf unless she asks you to call 911 for immediate protection. Never underestimate the potential cruelty, vindictiveness, or deadly action from an abuser, and take appropriate precautions

- Never talk with the abuser, even if the victim asks you to, with the hope that you can help him change. Remind her that she is your priority, and she came for help, not her spouse

- Let the victim know that you will not tell her spouse about the meeting because it is confidential.

3. **Believe the Victim:** By the time she finds the courage to say anything, she is at the end of her rope. Whatever the victim chooses to share is just the tip of the iceberg. No one shares the most horrible things with someone they barely know. It may take several meetings for her to open up

- When a victim comes to you, believe her

- Her biggest fear is that no one will believe her, which is exactly what her abuser tells her

- Victims must know that they are not crazy or stupid. They were deceived because they were missing vital facts about Christ's healthy love, God's marriage design, what is healthy, unhealthy, or toxic-abusive, and the types and signs of abuse

- Listen compassionately

- Don't interrupt

- Become comfortable with silence

- Give her the space, grace, and time she needs. You are the hope and Christ's lifeline she needs to untangle from her abuse and be free.

4. **Let Her Know What You Can and Cannot Do:** In Part 1, we stated our responsibilities. Faith leaders, it's not our job to fix, heal, save, or professionally counsel believers coming to us for help. It's our responsibility to know how to listen to them without dismissal, judgment, and condemnation and determine what kind of help they need and provide it in Christ's love

- Be clear that you are there to help, support, and teach her all the elements of Christ's healthy love

- Your focus and loyalty are to the victim. You will not talk with her spouse about what she discusses to keep her safe

- You cannot fix, counsel, heal, or save her. You are not here to tell her what to do or to be in the middle of their marriage

- You may offer suggestions, but ultimately, she must decide. Assure her that no matter what she chooses, you will support her through prayer and your willingness to help her explore what it means to live in Christ's healthy love

5. **Listen for Key Words of Abuse:** Most of the victims' statements and questions come from "I or me." Example: What's wrong with me? I try to do what my husband says, but it turns out wrong. Why can't I make him happy? Listen for these keywords:

- Fear or being afraid. "I don't want to make my husband mad"

- The need for permission phrases, "I can't _____ unless or until I ask my husband"

- "I can't seem to do anything right"

- Taking false blame for causing her spouse to get mad, blow up, etc. She may say, "I know he loves me, but he's so stressed, he's had a hard life, he needs to let off steam, etc." She uses rationales or excuses to justify his disrespectful words and hurtful behavior and to try to make sense of what is going on

- She questions why he says he's sorry, but he continues to hurt her

- If I were a better wife, then he would or wouldn't _____

- He says I need to _____ and then he would not get mad

- If I would _____ then he would (love me more, be more attracted to me, etc.)

- I keep praying for God to heal my marriage, but nothing is changing. I guess I'm supposed to stay here until God does something

- My hard marriage is my punishment for my past. I deserve this, but it is so hard. How can I fix this?

- My husband has a good heart, and there are some really good times, so why are the bad times so bad?

- If my husband says he loves God and he serves in the church and community, why does he say mean things and hurt me?

- I believe God can heal my husband if I just learn how to help him or I know what to fix in myself

Some nonverbal signs:

- Looks defeated

- Afraid to look you in the eye

- Extremes of not taking care of themselves or looking picture perfect

- Wears long sleeves when it's hot outside

- Pulling at or arranging clothes to hide bruises

- Checking the time and acting nervous, or any other signs

6. **Practice Empathetic, Active, and Reflective Listening:** Listen for several key points you can repeat back to her in her own words. Here is an example of reflective and empathetic listening. If you hear a lot of fear, you can say, "It sounds like you are fearful when you say, 'I don't know what he will do and I don't feel safe.' Is this correct?"

Reflecting the victim's phrases helps her:

- See that you are listening and you care

- You believe her

- She is not alone

- Helps her validate her thoughts

- Keep her in the driver's seat of the conversation

NEVER, NEVER, NEVER ASK WHY! The question why suggests:

- She's to blame for the abuse

- She's lying

- She's responsible for fixing the abuse and her marriage

- You condone the abuse, so she must let it happen

Neither of these two suggestions are true or possible. What a faith leader says has a paramount impact on whether she feels safe, hopeful, empowered, or judged, condemned, and on her own. How she is treated greatly influences what she will do next, as you experienced in the exercise "In Her Shoes."

7. **Some Questions You Can Use to Give the Victim a Voice:** The victim's answers to most of the questions can ignite her emotions, so don't be surprised. When the victim feels safe and begins to speak her truth, the reality is hard and painful. The answers to these questions will reveal control, many or all of the tactics of fear, isolation, intimidation, blame, emotional abuse, coercion, the using of children, spiritual abuse, and the loving husband deception.

- How did you feel?
- Can you tell me more?
- Is your family close or supportive?
- Do you have someone who has helped you in the past?
- When you get sick, who takes care of you?
- What do you feel like right before your husband comes home?
- Can you tell me what happens if your husband gets really mad?
- What do you believe a Christian marriage looks like?
- What is your definition of love?

8. **If She Is Open to Hearing the Truth, Share the Types of Marriages and the Types and Signs of Abuse:** We have summarized information sheets they can look at in the Supporting Victims Guide Packet at the back of the guidebook

9. **Encourage Her with God's Truth in Christ's Love:** Victims are filled with doubts, false shame and guilt, and they have low self-worth. They need to know Christ's love first. They need verses for identity, self-worth according to God, marriage, and God's truth and Christ's power living in them. A larger list of verses you can share with the victim are in the Supporting Victims Guide Packet at the back of the guidebook.

Here are a few verses:

Identity and Self-worth

1 John 3:1, NIV	See what great love the Father has lavished on us, that you are called a child of God! And that is what we are!
Psalms 139:13-14 NIV	God created your inmost being; He knit you together in your mother's womb.

Marriage

Matthew 25:40, NLT	Jesus told us. "When your (spouse did _____) to you, he was doing it to me (Christ is living in you)!"
1 Cor. 13:4-7, NLT	Replace the word love with your spouse's name.
Example: Spouse's name _____	is patient and kind.
_____,	is not jealous or boastful or proud or rude.
_____,	does not demand his own way.
_____,	is not irritable, and he keeps no record of being wronged.
_____,	does not rejoice about injustice but rejoices whenever the truth wins out.
_____,	never gives up, never loses faith, is always hopeful, and endures through every circumstance.

God's Truth and Power

Matthew 22:29, NLT	Jesus replied, "Your mistake is that you don't know the scriptures, and you don't know the power of God."
John 8:31-32, ESV	So Jesus said to the Jews who had believed him, "If you abide in my word, you are truly my disciples, and you will know the truth, and the truth will set you free."
Psalm 18:2, NLT	The Lord is my rock, my fortress, and my savior; my God is my rock, in whom I find protection. He is my shield, the power that saves me, and my place of safety.
Isaiah 43:2-4, MSG	Don't be afraid, I've redeemed you. I've called your name. You're mine. When you're in over your head, I'll be there with you. When you're in rough waters, you will not go down. When you're between a rock and a hard place, it won't be a dead end— Because I am God, your personal God, The Holy of Israel, your Savior. I paid a huge price for you, . . . that's how much you mean to me! That's how much I love you!

10. **Encourage Counseling and a Safety Plan:**

- Let her know that the only person she can understand or work on is herself and the best place to start is with a counselor experienced in abuse. They can help her make the best decisions to stay safe

- Encourage her to call a hotline or the local shelter for women to create a safety plan in case the abuse escalates to a dangerous level

- Always have current referral information for counselors experienced with abuse, the local women's shelter with housing, legal, financial services, and the hotline phone number.

11. **No Expectations or Demands—Only Respect:** Your empathy needs to include that you understand her fear of taking these steps, but you are not expecting or demanding her to make any decisions right now

- Be realistic that without her actions and change, everything stays the same

- Let her know that you understand that learning and breaking free of abuse is a process of untangling many aspects of her life. It's like untangling a ball of twine with the help and support of others

- Respect her decision for what she will and will not do right now

- Let her know that she is the expert on her abuser and what is safe or dangerous

- Tell her that she is wise and smart because she has survived this long, and now she's seeking help

- If a woman declines help right now, respect her choice as she is the expert on her situation

- Assure her that your door is always open and she can contact you in the future

- Offer her the opportunity to learn about Christ's love on her own, with you, or in a Bible study from the book and workbook *Quest for Exceptional Love*. The first place Jesus met hurting people was in His love, and faith leaders can do the same!

12. **Boundaries:** If the victim asks about boundaries, you can confirm that they are good, but they need to be determined for her situation with a counselor experienced with abuse. Encourage her to seek help to learn more with her counselor and have the names of counselors available.

13. **Realities of Couples Counseling in a Toxic-Abusive Dictatorship Marriage:** Faith leaders are not alone in trying to find the best ways to handle unhealthiness and toxic-abusive marriages. An article, "Couple and Marital Counseling," on the Psychology Research and Reference website, states:

An additional challenge to couple and marital counseling is the prevalence of violence among couples. A call to the profession is to develop more programs for treating violence in the intimate relationship.

- First, faith leaders must remind the victim that she is not in a loving, equal partnership marriage where both spouses will do everything necessary to work on themselves and their marriage

She is in a toxic-abusive dictatorship marriage founded on power, control, and her spouse's ultimate authority

- Abuse is not a "couple's problem." It's an abuser's problem because only the abuser is choosing to perpetually sin against them, God, and their children

- The victim can't stop him, and she's not responsible for his sin.

- Never forget, abusers use the tactic of blame to place the responsibility of his abuse on her (the victim) to fix

- The abuser will use any means to convince the victim and other people that the victim is the problem

Putting the abuser and the victim in a room together is like putting a rape victim together with her rapist and expecting the rapist not to do anything to her when he takes her home. When the victim and abuser go home, she will pay for telling the truth.

If no one believed her and she endured spiritual abuse during the talk with the faith leader, she is left with more abuse while she tries to find hope and the strength to go on. Protect the victim and do not recommend couples counseling in a toxic-abusive dictatorship marriage.

- If the victim asks about couples counseling, tell her that she is your primary concern

- Help her understand the only person she can change is herself. Encourage her to find her answers first with a counselor experienced with abuse. Have a list of counselors experienced with abuse ready for her

- Let her know that most of the time, abusers let victims get personal counseling because they believe the victim needs to be fixed

- Make sure she knows that whatever choice she makes will be the best one right now

- Remind her that your door is always open and that you would be honored to share how Christ's love is different from the one she is living in

- Let the victim know that abuse is a Biblical reason for divorce and that she is not commanded or expected to be abused in her marriage. Make sure she knows you are giving her all of God's truth about marriage and that her decision to stay, separate, or divorce can only be made with God. Let her know that you support her, no matter what she chooses, because you only want to make sure she has God's truth and that she is safe

Abuse Is a Biblical Reason for Divorce

Let's read an excerpt from Joshua Sharp, author of Voices.

In Jesus' day, there was a fierce debate between two schools of thought within Judaism—the Shammaites and the Hillelites. The latter read Deuteronomy 24:1-4 as giving a man permission to divorce his wife for pretty much any reason. The Shammaites, on the other hand, argued that "indecency" in Deuteronomy 24:1-4 only meant adultery.

However, both schools of thought affirmed that a woman being neglected or abused by her husband had the right to receive a divorce, and Jewish courts could go so far as to beat the neglectful and/or abusive husband until he agreed to give his wife a certificate of divorce, thus legally freeing her to remarry.

In Jewish culture in Jesus' time, women could not initiate divorce and had virtually no legal recourse to protect themselves from being divorced. Divorce typically brought shame on a woman and left her economically vulnerable. Jesus' command actually served to protect women from selfish husbands who sought to throw away their wives like trash.[26]

---

26. https://www.baptiststandard.com/opinion/voices/abuse-is-biblical-grounds-for-divorce/
Voices: Abuse is biblical grounds for divorce. May 18, 2020, by Joshua Sharp

Reverend Al Miles, a teacher about abuse within Christian marriages, also summarizes why abuse is a Biblical reason for divorce.

> The husband, by his abuse, has already been "unfaithful" to the covenant he made with his wife before God: promising to always be a loving and respectful intimate partner. Acts of domestic violence destroy this promise; they demonstrate neither love nor respect. . . . In addition, it must be said that regardless of whether a battering husband remains in the home, he has already "deserted" his wife (and children) by his inappropriate emotions, physical, psychological, sexual, and spiritual actions.[27]

An abuser chooses to live in perpetual sin. He needs correction and accountability. HOWEVER, to hold him accountable and responsible places the victim (and children) in tremendous or deadly danger.

Therefore, to be part of the solution to stop the toxic-abusive dictatorship marriages in the church, faith leaders must focus on safely helping the victim. There are a multitude of entangled layers a victim must work through to make a safe decision. There may also be factors that we don't know that keep them there. Only a believer and God have the right to decide if she will separate, divorce, or stay in her marriage.

You Don't Know What Goes on Behind Closed Doors

Victims in unhealthy or toxic-abusive dictatorship marriages need our help! Faith leaders must know how to identify, support, and teach Christ's love to them. When there are frequent or overt abusive behaviors in a struggling marriage (more than two incidents in

---

27. *Violence in Families: What Every Christian Needs to Know*, by Reverend Al Miles. Copyright 2002 Augsburg Fortress, page 66-67.

a month or less), the marriage has crossed over to being abusive. It must be treated as an abusive dictatorship marriage.

The complexities of untangling from a toxic-abusive marriage vary from victim to victim. Faith leaders must never underestimate what an abuser will do to keep the victim under his control. Some victims choose to stay because of what the abuser threatens to do. The abuser's threat goes beyond bodily harm.

Imagine if your spouse coerced you into having sex and filming it because everything in the bedroom is holy. You don't want to do it. But with more threats and because you want to be an obedient, Godly wife, you concede. Years later, you discover your marriage is toxic-abusive, and you take steps to leave with your children, now eleven and thirteen. Your abusive spouse gathers all of the intimate tapes and threatens to post them everywhere if you leave.

Does the wife stay to protect her children from the humiliation she would endure from everyone she knows seeing these tapes? This abusive tactic is just another example of the terror that many victims must traverse, and sometimes they choose to sacrifice themselves to keep their children from more harm. What would you choose?

Until the church changes its perception, understanding, and the way it handles unhealthiness and toxic-abusive Christian marriages, the silent pandemic will continue. Jesus came to set the captives free. He came so that we could live in his fullness and healthiness.

Being a victim is a horrible, destructive place to be. Let's do all we can to support and help victims spiritually and teach them about Christ's healthy love so they can grow healthier and stronger in their faith, whether they stay, separate, or leave their toxic-abusive marriage.

It has never been nor will it ever be God's will for any unhealthiness or toxic abuse in any relationship or marriage. It's time to help victims and stop this silent pandemic of unhealthy and toxic-abusive Christian marriages.

PART 3:

ALL ABOUT THE ABUSER

The Abuser

In Part 3, we will cover the definition, mindsets, profiles, characteristics, and red flags about an abuser. A reminder: abusers are both male and female. Because the statistics state there are more male abusers, we're using the male as the abuser and the female as the victim. No disrespect or discounting is intended.

This section may spark some questions that will be answered as we go along. It may also trigger some emotions and feelings, and if you need to take a break or talk with a professional, please do so.

An Abuser

Webster defines an abuser as:

☑ A person who uses something to badly effect or for a bad purpose

☑ A person who treats another person with cruelty or violence, especially regularly or repeatedly

Before we look closely at the abuser, we need to make sure we understand what abuse is NOT and the truths about the abuser.

What Abuse Is NOT and Truths About the Abuser

☑ Abuse is NOT an illness or condition. Abuse is a choice

☑ Abuse is NOT "just the way he is." Abuse is a chosen sin

☑ Abuse is NOT caused by anger issues, although the abuser uses anger as a tactic to make victims fearful

☑ Abuse is NOT caused by alcohol or drug use. However, many abusers abuse substances

☑ A wife's love and God's love CANNOT heal an abuser. Only the abuser can choose to surrender and work with God

☑ An abuser's toxic learned behaviors and choices CANNOT instantly be changed or healed. Identifying and eliminating abusive behaviors and replacing them with healthy behaviors takes years

We have learned throughout this education that abuse is a learned behavior and a choice to sin against God, their spouse, and children. So, how do abusers deceive their victims and faith leaders? Let's look at the mindset of an abuser first.

Mindset and Characteristics of Abusers

I don't believe people start out choosing to become an abuser. Unfortunately, if they grew up in an abusive home, they learned about abuse firsthand. Let's review the statistics from the abuse section.

☑ Children witnessing domestic violence are abused at a rate 1500% higher than the national average.[28]

☑ Little boys growing up in domestic violence are 100 times more likely to become abusers.[29]

☑ 81% of men who batter had fathers who abused their mothers.[30]

It stands to reason that a victim of abuse at an early age chooses to become the abuser rather than risk being a victim ever again. This choice is subconscious as a child because they are trying to survive and make sense of their abuse.

Even if they were raised as a Christian, went to church, learned about Jesus, volunteered, or became a teacher or Pastor, they may not realize that they learned and operate in toxic-abusive behaviors. Their rationalizations and normalization of abuse come from five main mindsets developed in their childhood.

---

28. National Coalition Against Domestic Violence, Washington D.C. National Coalition Against Domestic Violence (NCADV). https://ncadv.org/STATISTICS

29. Senator Joseph Biden, Violence Against Women: Victims of the System (Washington D.C.: U.S. Senate Committee on the Judiciary

30. "The Effects of Domestic Violence on Children", N.J. Department of Community of Community Affairs, Division of Women

5 Main Mindsets of an Abuser

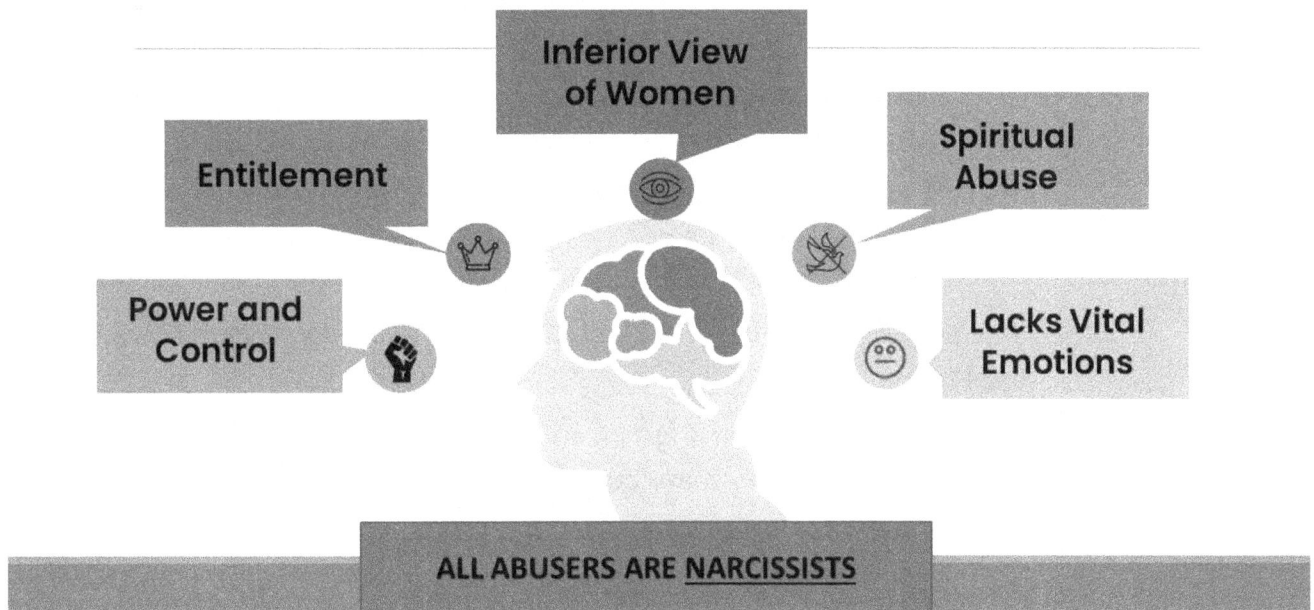

Inferior View of Women

Entitlement

Spiritual Abuse

Power and Control

Lacks Vital Emotions

ALL ABUSERS ARE NARCISSISTS

Five Main Mindsets of an Abuser

Abusers have learned to use their preferred sinful tactics to stay in control and power, fulfill their desires, meet their goals, and avoid feeling afraid and powerless. Abusers reject learning anything new that would threaten their falsely perceived ultimate power and control.

Even if an abuser proclaims to be a "Christian," they keep themselves as their ultimate ruler over God in their hard hearts because of five main characteristics in their minds.

1. **Power and Control:**
   - An abuser's goal is always to establish and maintain power and control over others through manipulation, confusion, coercion, blame, shame, guilt, or any other means.
   - Their fear of not being in control influences them to choose to operate in the perpetual sin of abuse rather than risk losing control.
   - Abusers use emotions as tactics to evoke fear or to play into the victim's hope by using the loving husband deception tactic in the cycle of abuse.

2. Entitlement:

- The abuser views his marriage as his kingdom, and God appointed him as the ruler.

- Abusers believe they are on the earth to be served, and his wife is responsible for satisfying all his desires and needs regardless of what it does to her.

- He feels justified in saying or doing whatever is necessary to fulfill his desires, accomplish his goals, and maintain control.

3. Inferior View of Women:

- Women are inferior to men, and therefore it's okay to degrade and use them.

- Women are possessions given to men by God to do with as they please because women are commanded to submit.

- Women are objects, so it is easy for him to discount and dismiss his wife's needs, desires, requests, or emotions.

4. Spiritual Abuse:

- Abusers repeat parts of sermons to support their ultimate dictatorship.

- Abusers twist God's word to justify their sinful abuse.

- An abuser is a master at placing all blame on the victim and making her solely responsible for his sin and their marriage because she made a holy marriage vow.

5. Lacks Vital Emotions:

- Abusers lack or have very low levels of empathy, shame, guilt, or fear of choosing to speak, act, and live in the perpetual sin of abuse. They choose not to learn these emotions.

- BUT an abuser knows how to act out these characteristics when it plays to his advantage.

- Abusers use every emotion as a tool in their portfolio of abuse to keep people thinking that he is a loving, caring, wonderful husband.

All of these main characteristics are in the definition of a narcissistic or a self-focused person willing to do whatever they want to fulfill all their desires and achieve their goals, without regard for anyone else's feelings or well-being. So, how do they deceive so many people? Let's look at the two main personality types of victims an abuser focuses on.

Abusers Look for Two Main Personality Types in Victims

Faith leaders must remember what we learned in Part 1. We all operate from our imperfect definition and understanding of love at first, and we are not taught the types and signs of abuse. Therefore, we are all vulnerable to the manipulative tactics of an abuser. However, there are two types of personalities that are prevalent among victims.

A) A loving, caring, and confident person who helps people.

- A loving victim may come from a healthy family, and her desire is to help others.

- The victim believes that if she loves and cares for someone, especially in God's love, the person can be healed and become a wonderful, loving spouse.

- Her confidence and spirit can be the challenge the abuser is looking to break.

- Helping others is a good trait. However, if she doesn't know anything about unhealthiness or abuse tactics, she is vulnerable to being deceived.

B) A person who is quiet, protective, wounded, insecure, rejected, or tries to be a wallflower. The person with these characteristics is dealing with voids in many of her ultimate needs we talked about in Part 1, to feel safe, loved, valued, belong, and have a purpose.

At eighteen, although I was outgoing, I felt love-starved and without much worth. When an abusive, young man paid me compliments, gave me gifts, and focused on me, I was ecstatic that someone loved me, but I was also deceived.

Abusers are wolves in sheep's clothing. To help us see their true character, let's look at the top three profiles of abusers, all of which I encountered in my three abusive marriages.

Top Three Profiles of Abusers

All abusers are masters of mind games and many other tactics to lure a victim into a toxic-abusive marriage. Their tactics will seem selfless or needy at first but beware. An abuser's motives are always self-serving and all about establishing and maintaining power and control over the victim. Abusers use a victim's unawareness, the voids in her ultimate needs, and her desires to love people to manipulate a victim. Let's look at the tactics of each profile.

1. **Mr. Wonderful:**
   - An abuser uses his charisma, position, and persona of "Mr. Wonderful" or the "fun guy" to manipulate a victim and other people
   - The abuser is charming, fun, or the guy everyone loves, full of compliments and showering the victim with gifts

2. **The Bad or Exciting Guy:**
   - An abuser is the bad boy or a man of exciting contrasts
   - The abuser has a dangerous, rough, or influential side and an exciting or secret side of tenderness he uses to entice the victim into believing that she can tame him with her love
   - This marriage is all about the extreme highs and lows of fighting and making up
   - The abuser can also appear confident and strong at first. But then he becomes a ruthless drill Sergeant and dictator

3. **The Hurt Puppy:**
   - The abuser comes across as a hurt puppy who has had a tough past
   - The abuser portrays himself as a victim because people don't understand him or give him a fair chance

The abuser plays on the empathy of a victim and tells her that if he had all her love and attention, they would be happy, whole, and healed.

All three profiles and characteristics exhibit the rollercoaster cycle of abuse as they switch from Dr. Jekyll to Mr. Hyde to maintain power and control. Every abuser chooses to keep themselves their ultimate authority, idol, and god. So, how can you tell when a relationship starts out good but, in reality, it is an unholy charade for a toxic-abusive one? Let's look at some characteristics and signs of an abuser.

List of Abusive Characteristics and Signs

☑ The abuser will overwhelm the victim with good words, actions, or things at first to make her feel like the most important person in his life.

☑ The abuser gives the victim more compliments than she's ever received and treats her like a queen to get her to trust him.

☑ The abuser tells the victim that she's such a good listener and understands him like no one has before

☑ The abuser moves the relationship very fast with the rationales; you know when you've met your soulmate or true love, so why waste time?

☑ The abuser slowly starts monopolizing the victim's time and spends every minute possible with her

☑ If a victim has difficult relationships with her family, the abuser will use them as an excuse for her to avoid them. He says that he is protecting her because she doesn't deserve mistreatment. However, this spills into all her relationships, creating isolation

☑ The abuser tells her how lucky he is to have her by his side, and he often tells people how beautiful his woman is. He shows her off like an arm trophy

☑ The abuser glares at other men or may even make rude comments, with the rationale that he is protecting her. As their relationship continues, he accuses her of flirting or having affairs

☑ The abuser begins asking more detailed questions about who she talked to and where she was every minute of the day

☑ The abuser asks the victim for favors to help him out without regard for her responsibilities or needs

These are just a few ways an abuser begins to invade the mind, heart, and life of a victim. Each one of these tactics at first fills a void in one of her ultimate needs to feel safe, loved, valued, and like she belongs and has a purpose.

When believers don't know the voids in our ultimate needs, that we are operating from our imperfect definition of love, what is healthy, unhealthy, or toxic, or the types and signs of abuse, we are vulnerable.

What Churches Must Know About Abusers

Never forget this image of a toxic-abusive dictatorship marriage. The picture reveals the struggle for the victim to be seen, believed, supported, and helped. Faith leaders must not be distracted or deceived by the toxic abuser who doused his "loved ones" with the destructive lighter fluid of abuse and lit their marriage and home on fire.

Christ's focus was always on the wounded, lost, marginalized, and victimized, and faith leaders must follow his example. The victims are the ones asking for help, and they are the people we must focus on.

As you learned in Part 2, faith leaders must make sure they don't do anything to jeopardize the victim or her children's safety when she reveals her abuse and abuser. Faith leaders must be aware and prepared to see the red warning flags revealing the schemes the abuser will use to get information from you. Let's look at the red warning flags.

Red Flags: Warnings of an Abuser

Abusers have refined their tactics of deception over many years. They are experts, and faith leaders must never forget this fact. Remember, abuse is a learned behavior and a choice to perpetually sin by the abuser. Therefore, this is a personal problem only the abuser can change.

Recognize an Abusers Language

☑ An abuser uses keywords that indicate his hard heart and tactics

☑ An abuser may begin a conversation by wanting to fix his marriage and even admitting to not being perfect or losing his temper. However, he will use the words "but," "if," and "she" with blame or rationales. Examples:

- Their marriage would be better if she would only _____
- She is too emotional, unstable, _____
- All his language will turn to blame, shame, rationale, or justification statements against the victim and others. It's never his fault

Red Flag Tactics of an Abuser

☑ If the abuser suspects the victim has talked to you or the victim tells the abuser she has, and he asks you what she said, respond that all conversations are confidential

☑ When an abuser suspects that his wife has told you about the abuse, he may:

- Become very friendly and want to be buddy-buddy. His goal is to convince you that he is a great guy; his wife is lying: therefore, you won't believe her
- Start up a conversation fishing for information about your visit with his wife and how much you know. Do not mention anything, or you will shred the veil of trust and protection for the victim and possibly endanger them
- Come to you for "comfort and help" with the rationale or excuse that he had a bad childhood or is under great stress to blame, justify, and rationalize his sin of abuse
- Plead with you to counsel and teach him. Do not counsel him unless you are professionally trained. Refer him to a counselor specializing in abusers
- Confess trouble in their marriage and ask you to talk to his spouse to try to convince her that, "He was wrong, but he will change. He loves her, and he is sorry." He will often use phrases of true love, soulmates, Christ's love, a good Christian, a godly wife, or statements of holy vows, forgiveness, and other spiritually loaded words to talk her into giving him another chance.

☑ If an abuser confesses his sins of abuse, you can pray for him, acknowledge the mess HE has made of his marriage, and refer him to seek professional help. Do not accept any blame, rationale, or excuses for his choice to sin. There is no justification in God's word for any type of abuse

☑ An abuser will try to convince you that God has healed him. Tell him that you are glad he is seeking God, but he will also need professional counseling to help him. Offer him some names of counselors specializing in abusers. NOTE:

Living a life according to true repentance can only be seen over a long period of time. Learned behaviors must be unlearned, and that can only happen over time

☑An abuser will openly state:

- mental-health professionals can't really help
- Christians only need spiritual compassion and teaching for their life's problems, and that's the pastor's responsibility

☑Abusers that are revealed are likely to react badly once they realize their manipulations and mind games won't work. Be careful not to be alone with them or turn your back on them, physically or rationally

☑Abusers may accuse you of believing lies from his spouse and being fooled, weak, and not a good Christian or other degrading tactics

☑Abusers may state that you are a bad, unfaithful minister, Pastor, or Christian

☑Abusers may accuse you of liking or having an affair with the victim

☑Never forget an abuser's goal is to establish and maintain power and control, and you are just another person on his list

The victim's reality is seen in this image. The victim is the dog chained up and being constantly abused verbally, mentally, physically, sexually, etc. After so long, a victim may snarl or bite back in reactive self-defense.

Never believe allegations from the abuser that the victim is also abusive because they have yelled, said bad things, or even thrown something at the abuser. Many people, including the police, misunderstand the realities of the constant torture of abuse that leads a victim to REACT in self-defense because they are just trying to survive.

Can an Abuser Be a Christian?

You have seen an overview of an abuser by learning the definition, mindsets, profiles, characteristics, and signs of an abuser. The reality is that anyone can profess to be a "Christian." However, not all who profess to follow God's ways have genuinely accepted Jesus as their Lord and Savior.

God has told us some hard truths that can't be disputed but must be understood. First, no one but God can or has the authority to judge an abuser's salvation or heart. However, Jesus tells us several times that we must evaluate a person, including our spouses, by their fruits.

> A good tree produces good fruit, and a bad tree produces bad fruit. A good tree can't produce bad fruit, and a bad tree can't produce good fruit. So every tree that does not produce good fruit is chopped down and thrown into the fire. Yes, just as you can identify a tree by its fruit, so you can identify people by their actions. (Matt. 7:17-20, NIV)

John, a brother, and disciple of Jesus, also tells us what it means to be a true disciple of Christ.

> Those who have been born into God's family do not make a practice of sinning, because God's life is in them. So they can't keep on sinning, because they

are children of God. So now we can tell who are children of God and who are children of the devil. Anyone who does not live righteously and does not love other believers does not belong to God. (1 John 3:9-10, NLT)

Difference Between a True Disciple of Christ and an Abuser

The difference between an abuser and a disciple of Christ is summed up in the following statements.

- ☑ A true disciple of Jesus walks hand-in-hand with Him and **occasionally** sins. The majority of fruit in their lives reveals love, joy, peace, patience, goodness, kindness, gentleness, faithfulness, and self-control. They display the heart and character of Christ.

- ☑ An abuser **chooses to perpetually sin** in abuse to maintain power and control in their lives and in the lives of those they profess to love, regardless of the devastation it costs. They are their own god. Their fruits are hurtful, manipulating, and destructive.

What About Christ's Forgiveness?

We will sin because we are imperfect. Jesus forgives our sins when we come in sincere repentance. True repentance includes working with him to transform our minds and actions to become more like him and move away from continually sinning.

When Jesus struck Paul down on the road to Damascus, Paul had to make a choice to surrender and work with Jesus in complete obedience. Faith requires our choice to believe and obey with actions. Being Christ's disciple means that you are constantly seeking, learning, living in complete repentance, surrendering to God's will and ways, and mirroring the attitudes, words, and actions of Jesus.

Abusers continually and deliberately choose to scheme in the sin of abuse. Their premeditation of abuse is not true repentance. They're not turning away from their sinful acts of abuse and working with Jesus. How can they be his disciple without living in surrender, true repentance, and obedience to God? How can they claim to follow Christ and act like the devil?

The Difference Between Spouse Abuse and Substance Abusers

In this training, it's vital that we don't confuse spouse abusers with people who struggle with substance abuse or addictions. Although an abuser may use a substance, which can increase the abuse, we must understand that these are two separate issues, according to Dr. Jeanne King, Ph.D., and domestic abuse consultant.

> In the case of alcohol and drug abuse, be mindful that the addiction is toward the substance. Whereas, domestic abuse has more to do with an addiction to controlling one's partner in and of itself. Addictions must be treated separate from partner abuse.[31]

An abuser will use a substance as an excuse for the abuse, but it is actually just another tactic in his tool chest. Faith leaders must always remember that abuse is a sin and a choice to maintain the powerful feelings of control at any cost through various types of abuse.

The Realistic Reformation of an Abuser

One of the best books on abusive marriages within the church and a "must-read" is *Unholy Charade, Unmasking the Domestic Abuser in the Church* by Jeff Crippen with Rebecca Davis. Jeff has been a Pastor for over thirty years and an expert on abusive marriages. He helps us understand how to help victims and how abusers can deceive faith leaders. His vast experience with victims and abusers gives us his alarming insights.

> Abuse is a willful habitual, unrepentant, hardhearted, hypocritical sin. Abusers do not change. What I mean by this is that cases of genuine, heart transformation of an abuser into not only a non-abuser, but into a person who actively loves the one they used to torment and works to expose abuse—such cases are so very rare that I believe it is unwise for an abuse victim to base her decisions and thinking on the hope that "maybe he'll change."

> In an abuser—with his utter self-centeredness and justification of his wrong actions, his lack of love for others and mindset of entitlement—all of these characteristics shout out loud that it is impossible for him to be a real Christian. Scripture clearly states that a person who lives for entitlement, power, control, and justification is not in Christ and Christ is not in him.

> If an abuser is treated as a real Christian who simply falls and struggles rather than as a person who has never known Christ, then the victim and other Christians will be confused about what it means to be a Christian. They will be led to think that abuse does not represent the abuser's true character, when in fact it does. The abuser himself will be escorted on his way to hell with his church's glib assurance that he really is a child of God.[32]

---

31. https://www.preventabusiverelationships.com/articles/sex_alcohol_abuse_374.php, Abuse and Addiction - What Is the Difference Between Sexual Abusers, Substance Abusers and Partner Abusers? Author Dr. Jeanne King, Ph.D

32. *Unholy Charade, Unmasking the domestic abuser in the church,* by Jeff Crippen with Rebecca Davis Page 127. Justice Keepers Publishing, copyright 2015.

Only the abuser can choose to work with Jesus, be transformed, and stop abusing. The abuser will need to completely surrender all his desires and practices of power and control in every aspect of his life and follow Christ's sacrificial ways. He will need to learn and implement healthy behaviors with support and accountability for years.

God's word tells us that His children will:

☑ Prove by the way you live that you have repented of your sins and turned to God. (Matt. 3:8, NLT)

☑ Jesus tells us that we cannot serve two masters. (Matt. 6:24)

Although we cannot and must not judge a person's salvation, we must evaluate their heart and character by their fruits of attitudes, words, and actions. We are called to be wise, beware of wolves in sheep's clothing, and test everything next to God's word, character, and the life of Christ.

The question remains, how can a child of God and disciple of Jesus Christ continually choose to sin in abuse? Only the abuser can choose to work with Jesus to change. Healing and relearning the healthy love of Christ takes many years. In the meantime, faith leaders must focus on the victims coming to them for help and teach them Christ's healthy love, so they can break the cycle of abuse in their families.

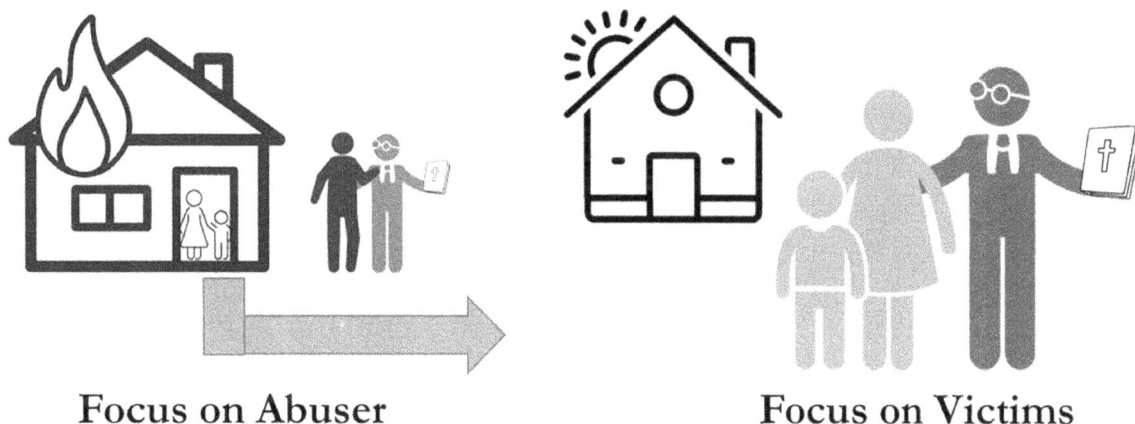

Focus on Abuser   Focus on Victims

Stop Repeating Pain

Historically, the church has primarily focused on preventing divorces without investigating or acknowledging why they happen. As we learned in the marriage section, a toxic-abusive dictatorship marriage is unbiblical, destructive, and the opposite of Christ's love, character, and example.

The moment a husband starts abusing his wife, he breaks his marriage vows under God to love, cherish, protect, and provide for his wife. Jesus did not call us to comfort, empathize with, or enable abusers who choose to sin in abuse perpetually. He tells us to hold them accountable. However, confronting or holding the abuser accountable can be deadly for the victim in the realities of a toxic-abusive marriage.

According to all the statistics you have learned, the body of Christ can no longer pretend that there is not an unhealthy and toxic-abusive marriage pandemic within our churches. What the church has been doing with believers struggling in their marriage has not worked. Unhealthy or abusive actions or a lack of actions do not follow God's heart or design of marriage, characteristics, or commands.

Nothing will ever change until you change what you know and put it into practice. The realities of COVID and the statistics and outcry from abuse victims, which rose 33-48%

worldwide in 2020,[33] have placed faith leaders in a unique position to speak God's truth, help victims, and put an end to future generations of abuse.

You have spent time learning how we have all been deceived by what we don't know. You have learned the hard truths and realities about operating in an imperfect definition of love, how our ultimate needs affect us, the types of marriages, and not all marriages are loving partnerships. You have also learned the types, signs, and devastation of abuse, realities of a victim, and the deception of an abuser.

Now, you have the chance to teach all believers the elements of Christ's love while you identify, support, and help the victims that come to you. You have the education and resources to follow Christ's example.

> The Spirit of the Lord is upon me; he has appointed me to preach Good News to the poor; he has sent me to heal the brokenhearted and to announce that captives shall be released and the blind shall see, that the downtrodden shall be freed from their oppressors, and that God is ready to give blessings to all who come to him. (Luke 4:18, TLB)

Let us be God's light, hope, and power to end the unhealthy and toxic-abusive marriage pandemic in the church by becoming part of Christ's solution. Let's explore an example of steps you can take to move forward.

---

33. https://www.ncbi.nlm.nih.gov/pmc/articles/PMC7264607/, National Library of Medicine. PMCID: PMC7264607, PMID: 32314526, Family violence and COVID-19: Increased vulnerability and reduced options for support Kim Usher, AM, RN PhD FACMHN, 1 Navjot Bhullar, BA(Hons) MA, MPhil, PhD MAPS, 2 Joanne Durkin, PgDip MA, 1 Naomi Gyamfi, BSc (Hons) MSc, 1 and Debra Jackson, AO, RN PhD FACN SFHEA MRSNZ 3

PART 4

MOVING FORWARD

The Church's Proactive Role with Christ to End Unhealthy and Toxic-Abusive Marriages Among Christ's Disciples

Love and truth must be maintained in perfect balance. Truth is never to be abandoned in the name of love. But love is not to be deposed in the name of truth... Truth without love has no decency; it's just brutality. On the other hand, love without truth has no character; it's just hypocrisy.

- John MacArthur

The Church's role and responsibility with Christ are to become part of the solution to stop the unhealthy and toxic-abusive marriages in loving, safe ways. It's time for us to acknowledge our challenges, educate all believers, find and develop resources, and teach everyone how to love others as Jesus Christ loves us. Through this fundamental teaching, you have learned:

- ☑ God's children will continue to operate from their imperfect definition of love by default unless they learn and implement Christ's definition of love in their lives

- ☑ Believers need to understand the lies they believe about love, marriage, abuse, and how they were deceived by the voids in their ultimate needs and mistaken identity

- ☑ We can no longer assume or treat all marriages as loving, equal partnerships because some marriages are toxic-abusive dictatorships

- ☑ We must listen to the person coming to us for help, believe them, and protect their vulnerability and trust

- ☑ It's not a faith leader's job to fix, heal, or save a believer's struggling marriage. However, we have learned to recognize if an unhealthy marriage is leaning toward being an abusive dictatorship marriage. Remember, there is a thin line between an unhealthy and toxic-abusive marriage. One unhealthy incident does not make the marriage abusive. However, if the victim experiences more than two unhealthy or overtly abusive behaviors in a month or less, we must consider that the marriage is abusive to protect the victim. The victim needs our support and professional help from a counselor experienced in abuse. If there is any question, always move to protect the person who came to you for help

- ☑ The realities of living in an unhealthy and toxic-abusive marriage are complex. It will take time to unravel all aspects of their lives safely. We must not place judgment or demands on them or abandon them if they choose to stay, separate, or divorce. We must stand beside them with Christ's compassion as they work through this challenge

- ☑ We have learned skills to identify, support, and empower victims to overcome their abuse in their timing and how to work with Jesus to live in his love

- ☑ We have learned the mindset, characteristics, tactics, and red flags of abusers so that we are not deceived

- ☑ Faith leaders can't address abusers in church without putting victims in grave or deadly danger. However, we can subtly open the door by teaching the whole church all the aspects of Christ's healthy love to help them recognize any contrasts between the love in their marriage and Christ's

All believers need a faith leader's support and guidance as they follow Jesus. They need to know that they are not alone, and it's NEVER God's will for unhealthiness or abuse in their marriage. Never forget that unhealthiness and abuse are a choice, and the victims are destroyed by the abusive spouse who vowed to love, cherish, protect, and take care of them under a covenant of God.

To help your faith leaders get started with your plan, we have created an outline with key points you may use to get started.

1. Have Support and Plans to Help Victims in Immediate Danger

- ☑ Our priority is to keep the victim safe and believe her. We must ask the victim if she feels safe and take action if she is in immediate danger. The victim will need to talk to the necessary professionals for help, but you can support her by being with her. I wonder what choices I would have made if the first pastor I asked for help believed and helped me instead of ignoring the abuse and telling me to submit to my abusive husband?

- ☑ Have contact information for the local women's shelters, police, National Domestic Violence Hotline (1-800-799-7233), and the Department of Justice to seek answers, resources, and help

☑ Encourage a victim to create a safety plan with a counselor experienced in abuse if they need to escape quickly

☑ Download your FREE Supporting Victims Guide Packet in Part 5 and use it when you meet with a believer struggling in her marriage. Find mature believers who have overcome abuse and are thriving in Christ's love who are willing to use this training and the Supporting Victims Guide Packet to help her understand what is really going on. This packet contains several lists, including a check sheet of the signs of abuse and other helpful information. I read this list when I visited the women's shelter. Facing my reality of abuse would have been better if I had a believer ready to pray with me

☑ Create or have access to community Christian support groups for victims and survivors. Because there were no Christian support groups in 1995 in my area, I had to attend a secular group. If I had been taught how to grow my relationship with Christ and work with him to heal the voids in my ultimate needs, I might not have ended up in two more abusive marriages

☑ Foster relationships with your local women's shelter and law enforcement

☑ Create and maintain a current list of local, church, and community resources: counselors experienced with abuse, housing, legal, financial, and career help. Many of these resources can be found through your local women's shelters

☑ Create and post a "grab and go" flier in all the women's bathroom stalls with information and a phone number victims can call for help

☑ Have information about abuse, your local women's shelter, and local resources mixed in a women's information board, so it's easier for victims to find answers and help anonymously

☑ Have a counselor(s) experienced with abuse ready to help victims and your faith leaders. I couldn't afford a counselor, I didn't have health insurance that would pay, and my church didn't have any free counseling or a counselor experienced with abuse. These realities left me on my own and still vulnerable

2. The Challenges the Church Must Meet

☑ Let go of past unbiblical assumptions, beliefs, and practices about love, marriage, abuse, and divorce that enable unhealthy and toxic-abusive marriages within the church

☑ Create a group of equipped faith leaders to continually educate other faith leaders about healthy, unhealthy, and toxic-abusive relationships and marriages through workshops or online courses

☑ Have a system in place to take calls from people struggling in their marriages that puts them in touch with a trained listener from this training immediately or as soon as possible. If you have a counselor experienced with abuse on staff, this is a great step

☑ Offering help and education about the signs of abuse posted around the church encourages anyone struggling in their marriages to call for guidance. Using these prompts lets believers know that it is okay if they have questions and that you are there to help. This information may help many victims realize that they are not crazy, they can find help, and that God NEVER condones abuse

☑ Help prevent future toxic-abusive marriages by facilitating classes onsite or online about all the elements of Christ's healthy love and the types and signs of healthy, unhealthy, and abusive relationships for women, men, singles, college-age, teenagers, pre-marriage, married couples, and divorced. One resource is Quest for Exceptional Love, on www.amazon.com. I came from an unhealthy home, even though both of my parents loved God. Because of their unhealthiness, I had no clue what healthy love looked like. What could have been different if I had been taught the difference between my imperfect definition of love compared to Christ's healthy characteristics of love?

3. Education from the Pulpit

☑ When you talk about love, relationships, and marriage in sermons and throughout your ministries, will you stand on God's truth and state that abuse is NEVER God's will and it is not in His design for marriage or any relationship? I can't tell you how many times my heart has hurt, and I've seen other people (victims) hurt when a pastor ignores, dismisses, or excuses unhealthiness, toxicity, or abuse because you are married and you just need to work it out

☑ How can you add examples of how a partnership marriage differs from a struggling marriage to help believers realize that not all Christian marriages are partnership marriages? Use a "struggling marriage" instead of an unhealthy or abusive marriage to protect victims in your audience. By acknowledging two types of marriages and showing believers the differences, you give victims new knowledge of God's truth and hope. It's vital to have a phone number they can call if they are struggling and have a person equipped to help

☑ What language will you incorporate into your church's information and sermons that acknowledge unhealthiness and that abuse is never God's will?

☑ What language will you use or change to ensure all scripture is explained in the correct context concerning Christ's love and God's marriage design in healthy partnership marriages versus struggling ones (abusive ones)? You may have to have two examples so believers can see the differences. For years, I tried to follow scriptures and advice from the pulpit to have a healthy marriage, only to end up in more abuse. I didn't know that I was in a toxic-abusive dictatorship marriage, which meant any healthy advice would have the opposite result because the abuser wouldn't let anything change his control. Believers must be taught these differences to realize they are not the problem and they can make different choices

☑ How will you ensure your congregation has a unified definition and understanding of Christ's healthy love, what is healthy, unhealthy, toxic, a Godly woman or man, God's design for marriage, and any other definitions that can empower them to be like Christ?

4. Discipleship Classes to Continue Education and Growth

☑ Jesus came to people in his pure love and met them where they were. It's vital for God's children to be taught Christ's love because we all come from so many experiences and definitions of imperfect love. When all believers are taught the unified definition, characteristics, and standards of Christ's love and discipleship and how to apply it in practical ways, there will be less unhealthiness and abuse

☑ Believers also need to be taught how to study scripture, talk with and hear God, and all the other aspects of discipleship. TheNavigators.org has many resources that can facilitate studies onsite or through the internet. Can your church offer a series of discipleship classes in a sequence several times a year, so no one falls through the cracks? Whatever resources your faith leaders consider, make sure it comes from God's word and doesn't condone keeping women silent victims of abuse. My healing and revelations came from learning all of these aspects, especially learning how to study God's word, hear from Him, and who I am in Christ. Knowing how to be Christ's disciple changed everything!

5. Recommended Books

All faith leaders can prepare their minds and hearts to identify and support a victim while not being deceived by the abuser by reading the books below. Start with the three MUST READS and more.

☑ *Unholy Charade, Unmasking the Domestic Abuser in the Church* by Pastor Jeff Crippen (A MUST READ)

☑ *Quest for Exceptional Love: Transform Your Love and Relationships Through Christ's Love Design* by Darla Colinet (A MUST READ)

☑ *When to Walk Away* by Gary Thomas (A MUST READ)

☑ *God Hates Abuse: Abuse and the Doctrine of Headship and Submission* by Robin Mullins Senger

☑ *Violence in Families: What Every Christian Needs to Know* by Reverend Al Miles

☑ *When Helping You is Hurting Me* by Carmen Renee Berry

☑ *The Emotionally Destructive Relationship, Seeing it, Stopping it, Surviving it* by Leslie Vernick

☑ *Restored, a Handbook for Female Survivors of Domestic Abuse with a Christian Perspective* by Esther Sweetman. Order copies at www.restoredrelationships. org. A great resource for victims and survivors

☑ *Escaping the Maze of Spiritual Abuse: Creating Healthy Christian Cultures* by Dr. Lisa Oakley, Justin Humphreys, SPCK Publishing.

☑ Any other books that address the sin of abuse

This fundamental training was only possible through the revelations and healings Jesus has done throughout my life. The unjust treatment I received from some faith leaders left me feeling hopeless and helpless. However, all that the enemy planned to use to destroy me, God is now using to help others.

Although I'm thriving in Christ's love, my heart still hurts for my sons and grandson. Because of the unjust treatment I received and the abuse my sons endured from their dad, even though we went to church, my sons still struggle to see the grace, mercy, and healing of Christ. I'm doing everything possible to help them see what is healthy, unhealthy, and toxic-abusive. However, I don't want other victims or their children to endure this reality or pain.

Faith leaders, we have an opportunity of historical proportions to help end the pandemic reign of unhealthy and abusive marriages in our churches and future generations. With our new knowledge and understanding, we can help victims find God's truth in love instead of facing condemnation, being told they are required to stay in their marriages, and continuing to be abused.

It's time for us to be the loving help, support, and Christ's solution to end this pandemic!

Let's move the victims into God's truth and freedom!

PART 5

SUPPORTING VICTIMS GUIDE PACKET

Supporting Victim's Guide

A Guide for Faith Leaders to Identify,
Support, and Help Believers Struggling
in an Unhealthy or Abusive Marriage

Darla Colinet
God's Transforming Grace

Supporting Victims Guide Packet

FREE DOWNLOAD AND A PERSONAL REQUEST

Download a FREE 8 x10 Pdf of the SUPPORTING VICTIMS GUIDE to use in your church or organization. It contains the summary guides for the victim and the abuser, a checklist of the signs of abuse for believer's struggling in their marriage to review, the Abuse Power Wheel, Snapshot of a Healthy , Unhealthy, and Toxic Abusive Marriage, Healthy Relationship Equality Table, and a BONUS download of the handout, *Healthy or Toxic? What is the Health of Your Relationship?*

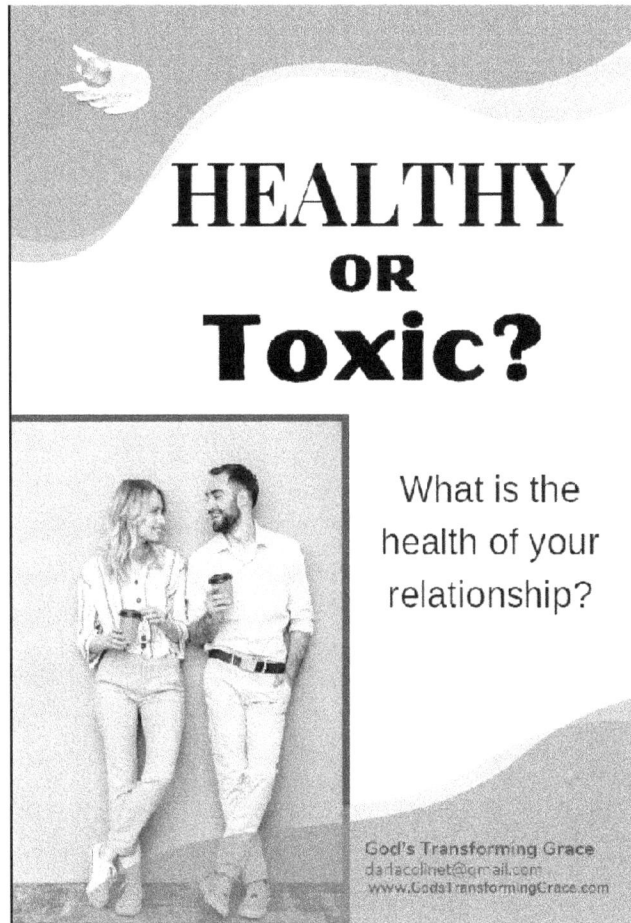

Go to www.GodsTransformingGrace.com. Click the tab resources – shops – products and look for the **RESOLVE1** icon. Type in the code **RESOLVING1GUIDE**, and it will be available.

Empower other faith leaders to help believers find answers about healthy love and marriage by leaving a review on Amazon for Darla Colinet.

ACKNOWLEDGMENTS

The creation of this book first came from the soft voice of Jesus in my spirit, calling me to help faith leaders learn to identify, understand, and support believers struggling in their unhealthy and abusive marriages. I know firsthand how vital it is for faith leaders to be equipped with the knowledge and understanding of the vast and varying complexities of unhealthiness and abuse in Christian marriages to end this pandemic.

I have taken the lessons in my life and what I have learned through various organization training about abuse and used them to create this guide. I'm so thankful for the beta group and our small group that helped me edit and make this guide a crucial tool for any faith leader, church organization, Bible school, or seminary. Faith leaders must know the differences between a healthy, unhealthy, and toxic-abusive marriage and the types of marriages and work together to end the pandemic in the church.

A special thanks to my wonderful loving husband, Alan. I couldn't have completed this book in God's timing without your love, support, encouragement, and help around the house!

Most of all, I thank God and Jesus for taking the ashes of my life and molding them into a guide to help others. Let me serve you and live in Christ's love in a way that honors you, God, my loving Father.

MORE RESOURCES FROM THE AUTHOR

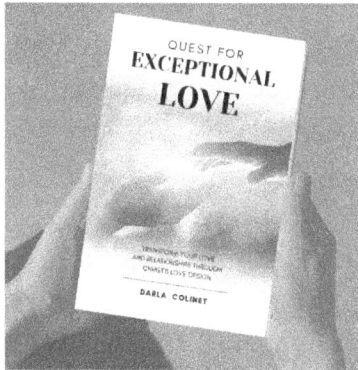

This book is a true work of heart. Darla takes her complicated and often painful experiences and shares honestly and boldly to help Christians struggling with their imperfect understanding of love in all relationships. Her ability to gently present the lessons she's learned and the truth of God's true and perfect love in her brokenness offers hope and healing. Come walk and work through this life-changing journey of becoming and embracing Christ's pure love design for your life. Embrace God's revelations as Darla shares her personal trials and triumphs in her quest for true love, for herself, and her purpose. In your journey, you may experience Christ's exceptional love for you! A workbook is also available on Amazon.

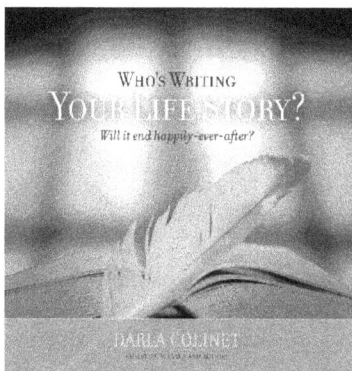

You are the author of your life! Your history and the challenges you face don't dictate your future chapters or final sentences when you walk hand-in-hand with Jesus Christ. This book shows Christians the source and solution to their frustration, anxiety, fear, uncertainty, and powerlessness through God's word. You learn how to use His wisdom and scripture to help you overcome the challenging internal battle between your sinful desires and spirit. You learn how to use God's armor to prevent the enemy from using your ultimate human needs, wounds, and temptations to destroy you. You grow your faith and stand confidently in Christ's power. Through Jesus, you can take control of your mind, heart, and faith and write the remaining chapters of your life illustrated with his abundant love, joy, peace, and grace and live happily-ever-after with him!

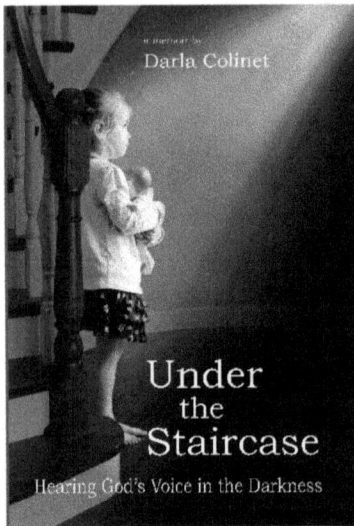

Under the Staircase: Hearing God's Voice in the Darkness is a spiritually stirring memoir of one woman's journey to find her self-worth despite the obstacles put in her path by her parents, her abusive husband of thirteen years, and herself. Her mother's depression and her father's long absences in her childhood left her feeling disconnected and abandoned. In a life-altering moment at age six, Darla found herself in complete despair. In the darkness, she heard the voice of her heavenly Father promising He would never leave her—a promise that became the unshakeable cornerstone of her faith when the rest of the world seemed to crumble around her. Holding onto the promise didn't make her life easy, but it did provide her hope and a determined faith when she needed it most as she grappled with the challenges of adulthood. Darla's story is an ingenuous and compelling tale of human vulnerability, the power of forgiveness, and the guilt that gnaws at her for not fleeing with her sons sooner. Walk with Darla through her life and discover, or perhaps remember, the light you have been seeking—a light that beams at the edge of all our dark places and gives us a reason to keep going, a reason to hope. A light that will help you develop a determined faith not just to survive, but to thrive in your life.

ABOUT THE AUTHOR

Darla Colinet is the founder and CEO of God's Transforming Grace. She is an inspirational speaker, author, and consultant who dispels the confusion and lies about love and domestic abuse through God's truth and Christ's exceptional love design. Darla brings hope, insightful revelations, and practical strategies through her authentic personal stories from thirty years of domestic abuse in three marriages. When she's not serving God from her home in Colorado, she and her husband, Alan, are off on their travel adventures.

Darla is a certified life coach and Christian coach and a member of the women's ministry core team at Timberline Church in Colorado. She is a consultant for churches and their staff to understand how to live in Christ's exceptional love design and to recognize and support victims of domestic abuse. Keep in touch and find out about my online classes and workshops at:www.GodsTransformingGrace.com

Support sharing the true love of Christ by joining my social media groups.

https://www.facebook.com/DarlaColinetSpeaker

https://www.linkedin.com/in/darla-colinet/

https://www.youtube.com/channel/UCMis2kfa-Hh_Y0KmAgbsPaw/

https://www.pinterest.com/darlatgm/

https://www.instagram.com/darlacolinet/

I would love to answer your questions and to hear your story and how God has helped you through my books. Email me at darlacolinet@gmail.com.

www.ingramcontent.com/pod-product-compliance
Lightning Source LLC
Chambersburg PA
CBHW080422030426
42335CB00020B/2554